ARKANA

Zen in the Art of He[...]

David Brandon is a psychiatric social worker and psychotherapist now working freelance in Preston, Lancashire. He is
the author of twenty-five books and pamphlets, including *Free
to Choose*, *Homeless* and, most recently, *Mutual Respect*, as
well as the editor of a national magazine, *Community Living*.
He was formerly Director of North West MIND and was
ordained as a Zen Buddhist monk in 1982.

Zen in the Art of Helping

DAVID BRANDON

ARKANA

PENGUIN BOOKS

Published by the Penguin Group
Penguin Books Ltd, 27 Wrights Lane, London W8 5TZ, England
Penguin Books USA Inc., 375 Hudson Street, New York, New York 10014, USA
Penguin Books Australia Ltd, Ringwood, Victoria, Australia
Penguin Books Canada Ltd, 10 Alcorn Avenue, Toronto, Ontario, Canada M4V 3B2
Penguin Books (NZ) Ltd, 182–190 Wairau Road, Auckland 10, New Zealand

Penguin Books Ltd, Registered Offices: Harmondsworth, Middlesex, England

First published by Routledge & Kegan Paul 1976
Published by Arkana 1990
10 9 8 7 6 5 4 3 2

Copyright © David Brandon, 1976
All rights reserved

Printed in England by Clays Ltd, St Ives plc

Contents

Preface

A writer is something of a thief. He steals quotations
and ideas from many sources. This work has
borrowed or stolen from too many people to provide
a satisfactory acknowledgment. I would like to thank
my students at the Hatfield, North London and
Preston Polytechnics for their patience and often
honest bewilderment.

My gratitude goes especially to Gillian Ballance,
Shirley and Alex Mendoza, John Pitts, Kay
Carmichael, to my wife, Althea. What little merit lies
in this book belongs entirely to the patience and
generosity of my Zen teacher, Dr Irmgard Schloegl of
the Buddhist Society.

I acknowledge the faith and encouragement of
Peter Hopkins of the publishers as well as permission
to use passages from my original essay 'Zen Social
Work' from the editor of *Social Work Today*.

1 Introduction

A wise friend advised against being clever in writing this book. He wanted me to avoid being too intellectual. He was afraid that I might drown the readers in a torrent of quotations from obscure Japanese and Chinese sources; that I might develop the whole Zen theme as a trendy contribution to the coffee table.

I have to travel light; to throw away my squirrel-like desire to gather nuts from authors who have written wisely and profoundly. The task is to dig deeply into my own nature and express segments of direct experience without inflating the ego or becoming intensely subjective. I want to write more from intuition than from cognitive reflection.

This means throwing away the desire to impress or to express ideas simply because they may provoke or sound good. Truth lies as frequently in the cliché and the banal as in the witty remark. I shall try to be honest and stay close to my direct experience. I shall repeatedly throw carefully contrived nets over the gossamer and elusive notions of Zen, Taoism and Nowness and hear the loud laughter of the Zen Masters as they cry out 'Live rather than define'. Zen Masters had a profound disrespect for everything — especially the written word. They were and are the Houdinis of conceptualization and philosophical speculation. That was their nature not mine.

Introduction

I have no intention of being bullied by the term
Zen. I wish to use it to describe a whole effervescent
flavour in living. I want to use it more widely than
simply describing a particular school of Buddhism.
About four or five years ago, it occurred to me that
Zen had much nutrition to give to my other love —
social work. The periods of meditation helped to
quieten my mind and enabled a clearer perception of
clients. It seemed that I could travel closer to my
own essence as well as theirs.

The nature of Zen does not lie in scholarship,
philosophy, in the Buddhist doctrine, and not even
in zazen [sitting meditation], in other words Zen.
It lies in one thing alone, namely seeing into the
Buddha nature that is in each person.[1]

This is close to what Quakers talk about when they
refer to 'the inner light in every man'. The
contribution of that idea deepened as the years went
by. The helping process is essentially about exploring
that light inside yourself and being a source, at best
unintended, of others finding their own.

At first, Zen had been a tool to satisfy the cravings
to become a 'better' person. I was more relaxed, more
serene. But very soon I was led to question the
ultimate source of this craving to be better. Why was
it so important to improve psychologically, to be
different, to change? Why did I have to deny the
darker side of my being, to be so dissatisfied with my
present condition? What drives me on so relentlessly?

Shakespeare's *King Lear* was an early guide. It
posed very basic questions about the nature of man.
What is man when divested of pomp and
circumstance, pride, social role and prestige, clothes,

lands and even sanity? Does an individual have anything special or unique, anything which makes his separation from others explicable?

Working with the suffering of the elderly and the isolated, first as a nurse and latterly as a social worker, the history of individuals seemed remarkably similar to each other and to mine. The differences seemed mainly cosmetic. At depth men and women went through broadly similar processes — the having of children, suffering and joy, facing sickness, bereavement and death.

Early in my social work career I became preoccupied with the problem of homelessness. These men and women had very little. They had been through the Lear process and divested themselves or been divested of almost everything — families, social relations, adequate clothing and money, proper food and shelter. I spent years talking to people who lived in derelict houses, under rail bridges and in parks. Little stuck to them. They were and are concerned with the immediate, the present moment and the coming minutes — the next meal, the next handout, the next bed.

It is no accident that so many of the world's great religious leaders chose to be drifters, to be without a settled home, to wander across the face of the earth. 'The foxes have holes, and the birds of the air have nests; but the Son of Man hath nowhere to lay his head.'[2] Having a home can mean a narrowing of vision; having too comfortable an armchair to travel anywhere in. Religious leaders have to float ideologically, to challenge prevailing and fixed views of life. The mortgage can easily be society's secret weapon against radicalism and iconoclasm.

Homes take people away from many of the great

waves and turbulences of existence. They are harbours
with central heating. They can persuade people that
life is warmer, less restless and disruptive than a view
out of a picture window will allow. To the homeless
such feelings are no insurance or refuge. Everyday the
homeless man looks for shelter from the wind and
rain. Everyday he is sensitive to changes in the
weather, to the different seasons. Life blows him like
an autumn leaf.[3]

The cost is unromantic. He pays for his
shelterlessness through bronchitis, frost-bite and TB;
through alcoholism and crawling fleas. He can readily
become an object of social charity, a piece of
plasticine to be kneaded and shaped by the social
services. He can persistently be defined as a
'malingerer', a 'beggar'. His sense of humanity can be
speedily eroded.

The primary condition for constructive restlessness
lies in following the middle way. To grow in mind and
body and to live iconoclastically, it seems necessary
to have neither too much nor too little. The poor are
eternally preoccupied with the pangs of hunger and
sodden with the rain; the wealthy spend their time
acquiring and protecting what they already have — a
state of satiation: adequate protection against the
winds of life. Only a man who is not imprisoned by
the weight of his possessions and yet not possessed
with the need continuously to find food and shelter
can ask and live out important questions. 'Who am I?'
'Where am I going?' 'What is another?' 'What is the
nature of life?' These questions and the living of them
are the nature of Zen — whatever you may wish to
call it.

Homeless men and women are great teachers. I
wish they had had a more patient and diligent student.

I found unlearning very difficult. I held on tightly to my sets of answers in situations where they became increasingly irrelevant.

In the following pages I shall try to avoid covering the trail with too many attachments, opinions and words, words and words.

> Alone in mountain fastness,
> Dozing by the window.
> No mere talk uncovers Truth:
> The fragrance of those garden plums!
> (Bankei, 1622—93)[4]

In this book I want to explore five major areas where the helping process can be illuminated. There are a particular group of people who help for a living — professional helpers like nurses, doctors, social workers, teachers. But all of us throughout our lives help and are helped. I want to apply the Zen blow-lamp to that process and see helping as a way of living and being rather than as a particular job or career. I want to object strongly to the aridity of much that passes for professionalization and technologization particularly in the helping professions.

I would be sad if this book were seen as yet another attempt at developing a helping superego. The way of Zen is not to reach out after our Superman fantasies, to explore feelings of 'being good' and denying our shadow self but to become more human. We learn to accept our fallibility; our anger and impatience.

I want to try uncovering the heart of Zen which is your own feelings and deep concern. This is a concern about intuition and compassion, much of which bubbles loudly in social work, medicine, teaching, in Christianity, the guts of Islam and the belly of Hinduism. Even though you had never heard the word before, you already know a great deal of Zen.

Hindering is rarely examined in relation to helping. In our hearts we know that we frequently offer little assistance to people and even, sometimes, hinder them. We demand that our clients suit our ideas of them rather than pursue their own pathways of personal growth — interfering rather than intervening. Helpers turn their clients into dependants; change them into passive consumers in what Ivan Illich calls 'iatrogenesis'. This simply means the capacity of helping organizations and helpers to hinder their users, to undermine their processes of self-help. Our craving for status, security and power conflicts directly with the provision of a truly helping service.

> I sit on a man's back, choking him and making him carry me, and yet assure myself and others that I am very sorry for him and wish to ease his lot by all possible means — except by getting off his back.[5]

The real kernel of all our help, that which renders it effective, is compassion. I want to discuss the nature of compassion. What moves our desire to help and heal? What is the relationship between our intentions and the results of our actions? This links closely with the summation of love and compassion — which in Zen is called Satori or enlightenment.

Nowness permeates the followers of Zen. It gives both life and energy. It relates directly to our notions of mental health — the ability to put the maximum of energy into the present moment is a large component of mental wellness. About the past I can do little; about the future hardly anything; only *now* can I make decisions.

Change is the hub of helping. We strive earnestly to achieve better conditions, insights, feelings for ourselves and others. I want to explore the implications and nature of Taoistic change, a change which begins from being rather than from becoming, a change which is as much concerned with our own hearts as with the situation of others and the wider social structures and institutions.

The last chapter is called Zen fruit. I want to outline the practical contributions which a Zen perspective may make to the development of caring services. How can we encourage the carers to challenge the basic nature of the services in which they work? How can we find daily nutrition in our ordinary lives? How can we constantly challenge current perceptions of reality from the basis of our experience?

2 What is Zen?

Zen cannot be defined. It is not a 'thing' to be
surrounded or reflected by words. When the last word
is trowelled into the prison it escapes and laughs away
on the horizon. As one of the great texts has it: 'When
we know what Zen is, we see it everywhere (and what
is everywhere is nowhere). How shall we point to it,
when it is in the very finger with which we are
pointing?'[1]

Describing Zen is like trying to lassoo clouds. Zen
is a Japanese word simply meaning meditation. It is
the name of a school of Buddhism stemming from the
confluence between the intensely pragmatic Chinese
philosophy of Taoism and Indian Buddhism probably
brought by the monk Bodhidarma to China in the
sixth century AD. It may well be that many of the
numerous stories surrounding Bodhidarma are myths.
Alan Watts even questions whether he actually
introduced Buddhism to China at all.[2]

The stories indicate an intensely enigmatic figure
as far away as possible from the conventional picture
of the religious missionary. He seemed intent on
provoking and annoying the Chinese whom he met.
He either directly discouraged students who came to
study with him or set them outrageously difficult
tests. This famous four-line Zen stanza was attributed
to him but was actually written much later:[3]

A special tradition outside the scriptures;
No dependence upon words and letters;
Direct pointing at the soul of man;
Seeing into one's own nature, and the attainment
of Buddhahood.

Whatever the historical truth about Bodhidarma,
the early Ch'an Masters (Chinese for Zen) were often
harsh, eccentric figures demanding strict obedience
from their pupils. They were great iconoclasts
challenging every orthodoxy not simply from words
but from the bowels of their being. Zen became very
important particularly in Northern China and even
more significant in the development of Japan some
centuries later.

Zen permeated and permeates many aspects of
Japanese life. Its influence and questioning about the
root and source of all life is seen in the freshness of
the paintings of Hokusai and Hiroshige. We can see it
in the sweeping calligraphy — a seemingly paradoxical
combination of intense spontaneity and vitality as
well as strict discipline. It is also found in bonzai
tree-growing, in gardening and landscaping; in the
haiku poems which blossomed from Basho and many
others; in the tea ceremony, fencing, judo, Aikido
but most of all in the sheer art of living.[4, 5, 6]

Zen was lived by thousands of Masters and their
students over many centuries. The living gave life.
Each Master handed down a liberating form and
message and a keen eye to the growth and
understanding of his students. The Masters were their
own men. Sometimes they behaved outrageously,
spontaneously. They pointed the way to
enlightenment; cajoled, encouraged and shocked their
students into seeing their own nature. These Masters

were practical men who mixed periods of intense meditation with cultivating the land to grow their own food and cooking and stone-breaking.

Zen is a way of awakening which makes no claims for a monopoly. The avowed intent is to set men free from their delusions about the world and themselves. Man is bound to the wheel of Samsara, the circle of self-frustrating effort. We are ourselves a part of the knot which we seek so desperately to untie. The more we wrestle blindly to untie the ropes, the tighter and more constricting they become. These knotted ropes are man's craving for sex, prestige, status and material possessions. He attaches himself to objects, concepts and belongings which weigh him down and prevent him from seeing the world as it really is. He is closed off from avenues of exploration and joy.

These cravings become cemented over the centuries into all forms of social structures and institutions. People who are relatively successful at accumulating goods and social position wish to ensure that they remain successful and are able to pass on such benefits to their children. They have dynastic cravings. Both in intended and unintended ways they erect barriers of education, finance and law to protect their property and other interests. They attempt to exclude the relatively materially unsuccessful from avenues of power and influence.

These structures and their protective institutions continue to exascerbate and amplify the basic human inequalities in housing, health care, education and income. They reward and encourage greed, selfishness and exploitation rather than love, sharing and compassion. Certain people's lifestyles, characterized by greed and over-consumption,

become dependent on the deprivation of the many.
The oppressors and the oppressed fall into the same
trap of continued craving.

These cravings cannot be satisfied in any external
way. The hole of wanting can never be filled, except
momentarily, by the objects of its wanting. As soon
as an aspiration or object is gained, I learn quickly to
discount its importance and another replaces it. As
soon as I have acquired the fast blond and the sports
car, I long for a large yacht and a country house.

These cravings are all mirages in the mind's eye. The
gap between craving and satisfaction is called
suffering. Man lumbers on in pain, pursuing attractive
mirages with no real satisfaction and experiencing
very little of the present world. Real awakening or as
it is called in Zen Buddhism, SATORI, lies in
breaking the bonds of craving wide open. This is not
to ask what will satisfy me but why am I continuously
unsatisfied. This is to realize the unreality of the
objects of desire, to explore your own wisdom and
inner truth rather than to seek outside.

Men search for strength, meaning and guidance
everywhere except inside themselves. We look for the
mysterious, the miraculous and the complex, never
being satisfied to see the meaning of our lives in the
simple living of it. We cannot see the truth in the
cup or tree.

Daisetz Suzuki wrote:[7]

Zen in its essence is the art of seeing into the
nature of one's own being, and it points the way
from bondage to freedom. . . . We can say that
Zen liberates all the energies properly and naturally
stored in each of us, which are in ordinary
circumstances cramped and distorted so that they

can find no adequate channel for activity. . . . It is the object of Zen, therefore, to save us from going crazy or being crippled. This is what I mean by freedom, giving free play to all our creative and benevolent impulses inherently lying in our hearts. Generally, we are blind to this fact, that we are in possession of all the necessary faculties that will make us happy and loving towards one another.

We already have all that we need however. The Satori of Zen is no distant magical or vague vision to be dreamed about but never really experienced in this life. It is what the Zen Master Nansen called 'ordinary mind'.[8] Its great wonder lies in sheer ordinariness — our own and the world's. It scorns the supernatural and the magical. It is equally at home in mud and pebbles as in the shooting stars and misty mountains.

Followers of the Way, the Buddha-Dharma needs no skilled application. Just be your ordinary selves with nothing further to seek, relieving nature, wearing robes, and eating. 'When tired I sleep. Fools laugh at me, the wise understand.' An old master said: 'Turning to the outside and applying oneself (to it) is a stubborn fool's errand.' If you master a situation you are in, wherever you stand, all becomes true; you can no longer be driven around by circumstance.[9]

If enlightenment cannot be perceived, it is because of its ordinariness; because we seek something special. Looking for the distant vision we miss the dead leaf on the ground. We seek everywhere but beneath our feet.

You should know that so far as Buddha nature is
concerned, there is no difference between an
enlightened man and an ignorant one. What makes
the difference is that one realises it, while the other
is ignorant of it.[10]

Each man is already awakened and has only to
become aware of this. He has already arrived at his
destination although he desperately attempts, out of
his unperceiving disappointment, to buy tickets for
further along the track. If he could only throw away
his fixed conceptions of enlightenment, the journey
would be completed. One Zen Master remarked[11]
'There is no enlightenment to be attained and no
subject to attain it.'

How then can the flavour of Zen be conveyed and
related to helping? It has the taste of hot chillies. The
mouth has to be wide open to permit the taste but
then it is unmistakable. We always knew it but had
persuaded ourselves that we did not. We know
immediately when good helping has taken place. We
have done ourselves some good as well as the other
person. At the time there was a complete lack of self-
consciousness or judgment. All of ourself and the
other was in the actual experiencing of the contact
and the merging of two or more persons.

The experience of helping had an internal harmony.
There was no longer a desire to play games or to
pretend. We had given up, perhaps just for a moment,
our attempts at manipulating, at impressing people.
We had forgotten our need to be important and
secure. We had forgotten our decisions about the
'good' and 'bad' parts of ourselves and others. It no
longer seemed necessary to define the limits of our
personalities and protect the boundaries of the self.

And even when we 'failed' in all this, it was also fine.

Zen in helping is nothing magical. It is that harmony which is common in social work, teaching and the informal contact between human beings. That contact melts away the gaps between the self and the other by being more fully human rather than through striving for the stars. It means taking down those barriers of knowledge, social position and education. It involves communicating and reaching out from our hearts aside from social conventions and expectations. It ploughs directly towards love through the minefields of 'oughts' and 'should bes'.

That reaching out comes not from a particular posture of professional position or even a study of Buddhism. It comes from our way of living. It is a direct recognition that although each of us is unique, all of us share the basic human feelings and experiences. We are born; we suffer and we die. Helping and Zen are not separate processes. They come from the same human drive to reach out to others, to make meanings and patterns out of our experiences.

Whilst a mental health social worker, I was called one evening to a house in West Sussex. The woman who phoned was in deep distress. Her husband had beaten her up many times before and she felt at the absolute limits of her mental and physical endurance. The three of us sat in a cluttered sitting room — myself, the bruised, black-eyed housewife and a silent, extremely muscular husband. She talked haltingly about their marriage. He was silent but suddenly erupting shouted 'I'll hit you. I'll hit you' and reached out thumping her hard on the mouth bringing her much blood. I said spontaneously, 'Hit her again and I'll hit you.'

She continued her story even more haltingly. A few
minutes later, he struck her another blow on the face
and I, almost simultaneously, hit him on the right
shoulder. He looked amazed. Social workers don't go
around hitting people. We talked for hours well into
the night and there was no more violence.

The following morning I sweated with all sorts of
cognitive insights. 'I am a Quaker pacifist. It is totally
against my principles and quite unprofessional to
strike clients. What if he sues me for assault?' At the
time, however, there was neither design nor reflection,
the action simply flowed. The morning after, an
ideological hangover, brought a sense of falling down
in some arbitrary human and professional standards.

The strongest flavour of Zen comes from the
thousands of frequently infuriating stories. My
favourites are about the Zen Master Bankei who
lived in seventeenth-century Japan.

When Bankei was preaching at Ryumon temple, a
Shinshu priest, who believed in the salvation
through the repetition of the name of the Buddha
of love, was jealous of his large audience and
wanted to debate with him.

Bankei was in the midst of a talk when the priest
appeared, but the fellow made such a disturbance
that Bankei stopped his discourse and asked about
the noise.

'The founder of our sect,' boasted the priest,
'had such miraculous powers that he held a brush
in his hand on one bank of the river, his attendant
held up a paper on the other bank, and the teacher
wrote the holy name of Amida through the air.
Can you do such a wonderful thing?'

Bankei replied lightly: 'Perhaps your fox can

perform that trick, but that is not the manner of
Zen. My miracle is that when I feel hungry I eat,
and when I feel thirsty I drink.'[12]

Bankei escaped from the trap the priest had
carefully set. He refused to match that kind of
miracle. He threw out the challenge of the everyday,
the sheer ordinariness of life in which there are
already enough miracles for any man.

It is easy enough to see the miraculous and
wonderful in things and people we regard as
important — in a ballet, symphony or love affair. It
is very hard to see something special in the
everyday — the washing-up or the gardening. Can we
accept and appreciate those things we decide are small
and unimportant? Can we wash ourselves with full
attention? Blyth writes[13] 'Mysticism uses the object,
the finite, as a telescope to look into the infinite. Zen
looks at the telescope.'

If we seek the extraordinary we are surely lost. If
we seek after powers of mind or body, qualities of
patience or goodness, which raise us above the level
of ordinary mortals, this cannot be Zen. Inayat Khan
tells a Hindu story.[14]

The little fish went to the Queen fish and asked:
'I have always heard about the sea, but what is this
sea? Where is it?'

The Queen fish explained: 'You live, move and
have your being in the sea. The sea is within you
and without you, and you are made of the sea, and
you will end in this sea. The sea surrounds you as
your own being.'

Zen is not separate from me or you. It is both inside

and outside. I am made of it. It flows through my
skin both into the outside world and also deep inside
to the recesses of my own heart.

There are brief moments when I become aware of
that. Moments of losing a sense of pain, of
fragmentation, incompleteness, of searching urgently
for something outside which will make sense for and
of me. My awareness of that process marks the end
of the experience. I can reflect that I was connected
to an overall unself-conscious rhythm. All the usually
discordant elements, the voices which expressed
various longings, came together into a great harmony
which was nothing special.

I was called to a block of flats in the early hours of
a wintry Sunday morning. Neighbours, hearing the
continuous cry of a young child, had rung the police
who, unable to gain admission, had telephoned me. A
mother had been battering her extremely retarded
child. All her frustrations at an absent husband and
the strain of a child not responding to maternal care
had boiled over.

At first she would not let me into the flat. We
talked through the heavily bolted front door. She
was terrified of her own destructive feelings, of the
bloodied and damaged child and also of the image of
authority which I represented. I felt her distress and
the extreme limits of the local government role
which I usually played. I seemed to represent at that
moment the worst elements of a self-righteous
community. A Pharisee of the Pharisees.

When I finally got into the flat we spoke hesitantly
for a short while before embracing and falling on to
the floor, crying into each other's arms for more than
half an hour. We experienced each other directly
without intervening roles and human games. They

were unnecessary. After crying, we talked long into
the night and the words were punctuated with tears
and laughter. I was very grateful to that mother. She
helped me to be more human.

Zen Masters used various methods to stimulate the
quest for enlightenment in their students. They had
to deal with two dilemmas — the quest for some
magical potion and the growth of ego which a false
spirituality could mean. One of the most important
methods used was the koan (literally meaning public
document). These were insistent questions given to
students to meditate upon and designed to burst the
ego. Typical were 'Has a dog a Buddha nature?' and
'Can you hear the sound of one hand clapping?'

Students had to focus on the seeming paradox of
the koans in their daily meditation practice. They had
to eat, drink and sleep with their koans in every part
of their everyday lives. Weekly they returned to the
Master and described what progress they had made in
their practice.

These koans are knockers to open stubbornly
resistant doors. They have helped generations of
students into an awareness of the narrow limits of
both language and conceptualization. Zen has no
grudge against the use and development of the
intellect. It is up to man to use fully every talent he
has. Some things are beyond the understanding of
the intellect and can be grasped only through sudden
jumps and flashes of intuitive thought and
comprehension. There is a gigantic distance between
knowing about and really knowing.

The symbols we use in language can become a
barrier when they are confused with what is out there
and inside here. Life is infinitely more complex and
beautiful than any of our words and sentences allow.

We cannot easily describe forces moving off in
different directions. What words do we use when
things are neither true nor untrue, neither black nor
white but both?

Words stumble after capturing the essence of life
which is continuously changing shape, always on the
move. They try to define the indefinable. They
resemble a sports commentator on the radio
continuously describing a football game which has
since changed. What we call paradoxes occur when
the limits of sentences to describe several
contradictory processes are reached. The Zen Masters
were too practical, too rooted in the earth to get
caught in those sticky nets.[15]

A monk asked Ma-tsu: 'What was the mind of
Bodhidarma when he came here from the West?'
Ma-tsu asked the monk: 'What is your mind this
moment?'

These koans and stories act like cold chisels on our
personal forcefields. We surround ourselves with
fences of electrified wire which rigorously protect our
separateness. The koans cut away at the wire until it
is possible for us to blend more with our surroundings.
The complete cutting of the wire is Satori — knowing
who you are. The knowing is not a knowledge about,
but a direct awareness of, life — direct
communication, direct awakening.

This awakening is seeing people as they really are.
It means seeing them with the eyes of love and
without the continuous carping and criticism which
is so much a part of my experiencing of others. Often
I can hardly hear what another says because of the
internal noise that goes on in the judging of them. I

have decided that they are too tall, too thin, too
angry or too depressed. Then I attempt to manipulate
them, to change them nearer to my heart's desire.

There have been a few times when my eyes have
opened, usually only momentarily. I have seen a
friend as if for the first time. For years my eyes have
been tightly closed to him. I had moved around
knowing roughly into which spaces he fitted, but, so
long as my needs were supplied like an automatic
udder, I did not have to look. Suddenly there was a
change and the milk no longer came through. This
changed my whole sense of security and well-being.

I had to see what had caused my discomfort. The
whole fit between us had altered and an emotional
draught blew in shifting part of my shell. I could see
the whole person quite differently — not only the
supply of warmth and milk but his sense of
desperation and loneliness. All those assumptions I had
been making fell apart.

For a moment, I would be clear of a system of
judgments. I would be so taken up with wonder of
just seeing an old friend that I did not have time or
reflection to form views as to whether 'this was bad
or good . . .'. 'I' disappears and decisions of badness
or goodness cease being made. Things simply are what
they are. The process of watercolouring the universe
with the poster red of anger and the green of greed,
in an arbitrary way, ceases. At this fleeting moment,
even the desire to be better, the longing and craving
for more of everything, disappears or is not felt.

Zen is a word to describe a particular school of
Buddhism. But Zen has for me a much wider
meaning than that. Like yeast, it bubbles and
ferments everywhere. It is joyous iconoclasm which
respects nothing and no one, particularly itself.

R.H. Blyth writes[16] 'to teach Zen means to unteach;
to see life steadily and see it whole, the answer not
being divided from the question; no parrying,
dodging, countering, solving, changing the words; an
activity which is a physical and spiritual unity with
All-Activity.'

He is describing a simple and important harmony
which underlines all things. But this harmony is not
exclusive to Buddhism which makes no such claims
for any monopoly. This flowing and bubbling is
found in many places. It ferments in the work of
Chuang Tzu, the Chinese philosopher; Meister
Eckhardt, the Dutch Christian theologian;
Krishnamurti and the New Testament.[17, 18, 19, 20]

I drink from that stream most willingly in the words
of the hermits and anchorites of the third-century
AD Scete desert. Those Christian desert fathers not
only spoke words but breathed and lived them
intensely. Their simple stories echo and contain their
whole being and faith. Perhaps very different kinds
of honest faith, attempts to live it out simply
combined with great discipline lead ultimately to very
similar places in mind and heart.

A certain brother went to Abbot Moses in Scete,
and asked him for a good word [advice]. And the
elder said to him: 'Go, sit in your cell, and your
cell will teach you everything.'[21]

A certain Philosopher asked St. Anthony: 'Father
how can you be so happy when you are deprived
of the consolation of books?' St. Anthony replied:
'My book, O philosopher, is the nature of created
things, and any time I want to read the words of
God, the book is before me.'[22]

Daisetz Suzuki saw Zen as a great universal building block.[23]

> Zen is the ultimate fact of all philosophy and religion. Every intellectual effort must culminate in it, or rather start from it, if it is to bear any practical fruits. Every religious faith must spring from it if it has to prove at all efficiently and livingly workable in our active life. Therefore Zen is not necessarily the fountain of Buddhist thought and life alone: it is very much alive also in Christianity, Mohammedanism, in Taoism, and even in positivistic Confucianism. What makes all these religions and philosophies vital and inspiring, keeping up their usefulness and efficiency, is due to the presence in them of what I may designate as the Zen element. . . . Religion requires something inwardly propelling, energizing, and capable of doing work. . . .
> Zen does this by giving one a new point of view of looking at things, a new way of appreciating the truth and beauty of life and the world, by discovering a new source of energy in the inmost recesses of consciousness, and by bestowing on one a feeling of completeness and sufficiency.

But the Zen of Suzuki is not beat Zen. It is not simply an excuse for following various arbitrary physical and psychological urges wherever they lead. It does not involve a *laissez-faire* attitude to living. It maintains a profound and disciplined challenge to currently perceived realities and values. It is far from passive and quietistic. It does not simply acquiesce in harsh injustices and do nothing about them. It is of the world not otherworldly.

The following of the way of Zen is disciplined and aims at increased responsibility towards others and an outpouring of love. This is a journey through an acceptance of full humanity not a denial of it. The height of Zen is a selfless compassion, a genuine love for both individual men and all mankind. Not man in an abstract disguise but in the distinct shape of the homeless man, the orphan, the lonely and the sick.

Love matters most. But not the love of doing good works or even of reflective and earnest political activity. This can simply be ego-inflating and expanding. Love flows from being rather than from becoming and cares equally for the oppressor and the oppressed. Love is without design or ulterior motives. Zen is a discipline of love, knowing not from where it comes and caring little about destinations. It always travels light.

3 Hindering

Thank you Master for teaching me nothing (Old
Zen story).

Traditionally, Zen has been without evangelism. It has
rarely tried to persuade people of its own merits in
relation to other religious schools, unlike certain
Christian denominations. People have come to it
largely voluntarily and with the motive to learn and
explore themselves.

Much of the professional helping, particularly in
probation, social work and psychiatric medicine has a
captured clientele. It deals with those who are seen
as threatening broad social values and may actually
(and frequently rightly) be very resistant to the idea
of being 'helped'. These clients may see such
assistance as 'interference' or 'controlling'. Every
society tries to process the small minority who are
viewed as homicidally dangerous or the much greater
proportion who seem to undermine established
social values and vested interests through their
delinquency or madness.

Until recently, the helping professions have been
buoyed up in a frighteningly optimistic surge. The
emphasis in their training has been entirely on
maximizing the potential within the would-be helper
for helping. There was much discussion about ways in
which the helped might obstruct that constructive

process. They might attempt to manipulate their helpers. There was no discussion about the ways in which helpers might manipulate clients.

The last few years have seen a great increase in people who felt that social work in particular was irrelevant. It had no impact on the daily lives of the poor and handicapped. It might even do damage by seeming to achieve something in a kind of public relations exercise. Now that feeling of irrelevancy seems to be becoming even more hostile. Radical social workers frequently see their profession as part of the problem rather than its solution. They have ceased to see it as helpful, grown out of viewing it as hindering and feel strongly that the profession becomes a hindrance to genuine social change.

The British magazine *Case Con* for revolutionary social workers argues that much conventional social work practice is lubricating destructive social processes which effectively exploit the working classes. Social work becomes one of a number of largely cosmetic methods whereby raw inequalities are concealed. Professional helpers 'cope' with the poor and handicapped and ease the pressing need for major social change.

Helping professions may be entering a period of acute self-doubt which can melt natural arrogance. Can we be sure that we help anyone, including ourselves? Is there such a phenomenon as the helping process? Can our efforts be aimed at reducing some of the hindering in which professional helpers particularly seem to be engaged?

We have all felt hindered by someone in our lives, although it is intensely difficult to define precisely. Often it connects with time. Someone devastates me with some insight, largely unwanted, which turns out

to be of lasting worth a few months later. A fellow
social worker told me some years ago in anger,
'Your affection is synthetic.' For weeks I became so
doubtful that I could relate to and touch hardly
anyone with confidence. Now I am glad that she
said it.

Remarks like that penetrate carefully presented
images and present real problems of integration. One
of the most important ingredients of mental health, a
very elusive concept, lies in this capacity to grow
flowers in manure. This is the ability to take personal
attacks, other people's anger and despair, as well as
your own, and synthesize them into new strength
and stability.

When we feel hindered, there is a personal
experience of hurt and injury. Our dignity, sense of
value and worthwhileness has, involuntarily, been
reduced. Sometimes we can be put off the scent of a
personal pathway of growth or be ruthlessly
manipulated or exploited by a person who seems
more powerful and knowing. We are left feeling
unloved and unwanted.

Sometimes that person intends us harm as in the
case of physical brutality or vicious personal attack.
Sometimes the harm may result from thoughtlessness
— it never occurred to the speaker that his words
would seem so destructive. This can be a symptom of
a sophisticated social game in which the speaker wants
to offend but simultaneously refuses to accept any
responsibility for it. Sometimes the hindering can
even arise from misguided love as in the 'Jewish
Mother' syndrome where the refusal to accept the
autonomy of the other is clouded with a mixture of
control, caring and power.

My first social work tutor advised me never to treat

myself at the expense of the clients. An important aspect of genuine caring lies in the continuing capacity to put oneself-interest second to that of the client's needs. We are striving for *his* greater independence rather than enhancing our personal feelings of power. There are at least two limits to this. Helping is not socialized masochism and the helper has also a right to satisfaction, joy and love from the process. Some individuals and groups, like the severely mentally and physically handicapped, can never achieve full independence.

Some people may not wish to tread the path towards greater independence. They may wish help in ways which we perceive as hindering both them and us. A client once asked me to help him commit suicide as he was in great pain and very physically handicapped. Such conflicts of interest and ethic require careful consideration. I refused to 'help' this client. Did my inactivity come from compassion or from some narrower conception of 'how he might be'. If after reflection the conflict remains genuine, as this one seemed to, we can tell the client so openly and, if he wishes, withdraw.

Both Bernard Shaw and Philip Slater argued that all professions are conspiracies against both the general public and their consumers.[1]"Those who seek to provide services are often prevented by established members of the professions — such as doctors, teachers, and social workers — since the principle behind any professional organisation is (a) to restrict membership (b) to provide minimum service at maximum cost.'[2] In an important sense that is true. Professions everywhere seem primarily motivated by self-interest which they are gifted in wrapping up as in 'the public interest'. The development of a healthy medical, social work, nursing, teaching profession is presented as if it were entirely concomitant with the growth of a healthy society. I doubt that very much.

At a practice level, the professional helper is daily split in several ways. He attempts to advance his own job security, car parking and office space and salary whilst providing a service to consumers who may receive less and less of his occupational energy. He treads a daily tightrope between the continual emotional haemorrhage and callousness. He has to continue to see his clients as people and to cope with the daily catastrophes of his chosen job — the attempted suicides, the baby battering, the depression. All these events stir powerful feelings in his heart but his own indisciplined passion may hinder effective amelioration of the client's distress.

He may feel other paradoxes. He works in a local authority department which stresses a service to the consumer and yet whose senior officers have actually very little contact with the general public. If he works as a social worker, nurse or doctor, his profession is meant to embody the heights of compassion and yet a considerable part of his task is to act as a valve between those who demand various services and the reality of scarce resources. 'Yes I do care about you. . . . No you cannot have. . . .'

The greatest paradox of all is the continuing and confusing shift between socially macrocosmic and microcosmic perceptions. The helper is faced with individuals in distress who are walking symptoms of major social inequalities. They suffer from homelessness, lack of adequate health care, lack of sufficient food and low income. By helping them directly the helper may hinder the development of constructive confrontation and possible change; by not helping he turns away from compassion and caring about individual people.

Fieldworkers can only do what they can do. They feel this sense of frustration and impotence often very keenly. Too many people have a view of helping as social Domestos. Unfortunately (perhaps fortunately), in our immensely unhygienic society helping cannot, like a good lavatory cleaner, kill all known germs. If the helper is honest, he experiences a thousand situations in which he can do nothing or very little.

By trying to be all things to all the people we can fail catastrophically. We are simply human beings. A recent book puts it dramatically in relation to social work:[3]

> Social work has become the unloved profession — unloved by its clients whom it has ceased to serve, unloved by the system that it has failed to reinforce, unloved by its peers whose respect it has lost, and, most poignantly, since it has not remained true to its own commitments, unloved even by itself.

Sometimes the struggle is not for the survival of the profession but more simply for that of the client and helper. Both feel increasingly overwhelmed by events. John Nurse writes[4] about handling distress and anger in clients. 'My temptation when under this sort of attack is to fight back, usually by endeavouring to get the client to take back into himself all the badness, destructiveness and fragmentation he seems to be trying to stuff into me.'

I have felt this strong urge to retaliate too. Some years ago I had a client called Billy, in his late teens, who annoyed me considerably. He would ask to see me and simply not turn up for the appointment. He seemed to be frustrating most of the small-town community — his parents, social workers and doctors by outrageous behaviour. He painted the local cemetery grave-stones, smashed church windows and gave local housewives instruction in obscene language. I remember saying aggressively 'Your real trouble is that you're a psychopath.' This created a great deal of stress particularly for his family who spent the next few weeks researching in various libraries for psychiatric textbooks and did not like what they found.

Psychiatrically, I was probably being strictly accurate. But humanly, I was using my own personal position to fire arrows at a patient. Those words did not contain a considered professional diagnosis but a provocation which released my frustration. I wanted to hurt him. I wanted him to experience how angry I had become. I put my own needs first.

One day, Billy told me he was going for a ride on his motorcycle. He had neither licence nor tax. The Beach area where he lived was a restricted 30 mph zone where a number of policemen lived. He was 'going to try the big machine flat out'. I advised against it. Billy cried 'You can't do anything to stop me.' I hurled his ignition keys down a near-by drain. That still feels right although it may appear in none of the professional textbooks. Billy learnt that I cared about what he did and the consequences for his family and also that I had a certain power as an individual. This time I was not trying simply to hurt him or to impress anyone.

Rosie was easily the most difficult resident in Greek Street — the community for homeless women where I used to work.[5] She was diagnosed as an acute psychotic. We were having an encounter group for staff in the basement which she continually interrupted by screaming and banging on the door. Later when the group members were leaving she attacked someone with a large broom. I was very angry with her and also anxious to impress visitors with our ability to handle 'difficult people'. I threw her out into the street which made her even more frustrated and angry. She kicked and banged on the large main door.

After locking the community door, I knew that she just couldn't be left to wander about and possibly attack ordinary passers-by. I went back out into the street and she attacked me with all her wild power. I forced her to the pavement and held her down kicking and writhing until someone called the police. A large crowd gathered and some of the men muttered about kicking my head in. They assumed I was sexually assaulting her.

A few months later, we had an awful day in the Greek Street community. Everyone seemed either to be stuffing pills or to be screaming, fighting drunk. Mary, in particular, was an absolute pest. She was demanding more than her permitted dosage of heroin. Every few minutes she would bear-hug me and I would shove her away and shout 'No'.

Eventually she began to overdose and threaten suicide if I did not let her have more drugs. The answer was still 'No'. In four hours on a busy afternoon, I found her near to death five times. The resilience of her small, twisted tortured body was remarkable. She slashed her wrists not very effectively; she threw herself down flights of stone stairs and bruised and bloodied her whole body;

she stuffed barbiturates down her throat and was
sick. Finally I found her with a stocking tied very
tight around her neck. Her bent physique was cold
with purple face. I got someone to phone for an
ambulance. When it arrived, not only had she
recovered and could admonish me with wonderful
vocabulary, but she point-blank refused to leave the
community. 'I'm not going to that bloody
hospital. . . .'

I carried her frail, racked, struggling body down
five flights of dark stairs. 'You are going to the
hospital, Mary. You are certainly going to go. If not
for your sake — for my sanity.' I felt fine about that.
I had taken all I could and there were no feelings of
scoring over her or trying to impress anyone. I could
feel genuine anger and frustration but still care about
Mary. Three days later she was back in the
community.

Ivan Illich has contributed vastly to our
understanding of the relationship between hindering
processes and the medical profession. His analysis has
profound implications for other kinds of 'helping'.
He has devised a term 'iatrogenic diseases', meaning
diseases originating from the physician. For example,
the United States Department of Health calculates
that 7 per cent of all patients suffer compensatable
injuries whilst hospitalized, though few take action.
The average frequency of reported accidents in
hospitals is higher than in all industries except mines
and high-rise construction.[6]

One neglected area, even by Illich, is the extent to
which we hinder ourselves. Are there ways in which
our practice of helping is used to stunt our growth as
persons? Giving to clients can be a very effective way
of concealing our deep-felt hollowness. I have

frequently heard myself giving advice, guidance and
love to people which I was completely unable to
give myself.

Helping and caring for others can be a very
effective way of concealing desperate personal needs.
It can conceal[7] a need to control and even punish
others. We may seek to be 'adequate in the face of the
inadequacy of others'. Throughout most of my
professional career I felt a continuing sense of fraud,
of not being worth while, whilst trying to
communicate the opposite to my clients.

Illich argues that there are three broad categories
of iatrogenic disease, these being: clinical, social
and structural. In the clinical category, the
professional actually damages the patient whilst
attempting to treat him. We have had a number of
examples, especially in hospitals for the mentally
handicapped, of physical brutality directed from
staff to patients. But in clinical iatrogenesis[8] the
damage takes place mainly either from sheer
incompetence or as the unintended and unforeseen
results of administered treatments like drugs. The
classic and frightening example was Thalidomide
which, when taken by pregnant women, resulted in
the birth of some malformed children.

The helper may further compound the felony by
denying any responsibility or by using his professional
shield as a defence to avoid the consequences of his
actions. In some recent examples of what looked like
someone's incompetence concerning the death and
injury of small children who had been battered by
adults, we have had social service departments, who
previously had claimed efficacy in the area of child
injury, refusing to accept a measure of responsibility.

How do we judge incompetence in helping? How

do we measure hindering? One major and general
difficulty is that of consumer evaluation of services.
A patient may be competent to assess the excellence
of his family doctor's bedside manner but by what
criteria can he assess the knowledge of particular
medical conditions or the skills of practice?

The practice of helping is so vague that it is almost
impossible to conceive of general measurements. I can
think of a number of examples of incompetence in
my own career. I was given wrong information by a
local authority social worker when enquiring about
adopting a child. I am sure that clients are frequently
given out-of-date advice about social security benefits
and aids for the handicapped.

Earlier this year, I completed a small study on
confidentiality among social workers. This indicated
that it was reasonably easy to gain private and
confidential information over the phone, whilst lying
as to who you were, from social workers about their
clients. Presumably such information might also be
available to private detectives and debt-collecting
agencies acting to the client's detriment.[9]

Geoffrey Pearson[10] looked at the misuse of
compulsory admission to psychiatric hospitals by
social workers. They

> frequently complained that they were forced by
> the intractibility of economic and housing
> difficulties into using psychiatric detention as a
> 'solution' to their clients' problems. And feeling
> powerless in the face of powerful and legitimised
> psychiatric opinion, social workers often went
> against their judgement in arranging psychiatric
> detention. 56 out of the 65 owned up to abusing
> the strict legal definition of the 1959 [Mental

Health] Act, but only two had actually gone
against medical opinion and refused to sign an
application for compulsory detention, even though
it is in the spirit [and letter] of the 1959 Act that
social workers should oppose medical opinion if
this is in the interest of the patient.

In the second category, social iatrogenesis, medical
practice sponsors sickness by reinforcing a morbid
society that not only preserves its defectives, but also
breeds a demand for the patient role. Remember the
song from the musical show *West Side Story* — 'Gee
Officer Krupke'. The young man and his friends are
trying to persuade various professionals that he falls
within their arena of influence and concern. 'Gee
Mr Social Worker — he's got a social disease.'
We develop a rewards system for taking on the
client role. The client status becomes the only access
to a wide range of different practical resources like
aids for the physically handicapped, monetary grants
and home-help services. He exchanges details of his
personal inadequacies for food tickets and financial
help.
The whole of human suffering becomes mechanized
and sanitized. Untidy processes like death and birth
are hidden away in special institutions. Young people
reach marriage and the entry to helping careers having
no direct familiarity with either. They have been
protected just like the young Buddha. This becomes
the first century to view human suffering as an
unnecessary evil. Our consumers cry out that they
are in pain, depressed and despairing. Usually we
attempt to alleviate their feelings, to remove pain
through drugs and professionalized comfort.
Is this relief help or hindrance? Many patients may

become addicted to the various anti-depressants and sleeping tablets given away so blithely in surgeries. 'How can I help you feel better' may in the long term prove to be less relevant than 'How can we work towards making you use effectively this feeling of blackness, aloneness?' Many trials and tribulations in life, including depression have constructive significance. As Anthony Bloom wrote:[11] 'Peace of mind is not absence of struggle but absence of uncertainty and confusion.' Perhaps our aim should be to clarify meaning and purpose in people's lives rather than dust DDT over the conflicts.

Patients and clients are encouraged to depend more on professionals who are seen as being experts — as knowing best. Social workers may see themselves as having an investment in their clients' lives. I recall one young social work student saying that the only serious personal relationships she made in her life were with her clients. One social work colleague refused to see a client again because she had rejected his advice on a previous occasion. He needed to understand the difference between advice and command. People must be free, in the great majority of circumstances, to accept or reject any advice given.

Michael Frayn comments on the growth of this emotional imperialism.[12]

No longer possessing the means to sustain any convincing social snobbery, we have branched out into moral snobbery instead. Novelists, critics, and popularising psychologists have joined forces to help the laity towards more 'meaningful' relationships and more valuable insights into themselves, towards 'realising their full potential as human beings'. We shake our heads sadly at

people's spiritual poverty, and smiling kindly, hold
out our hands to help them into better ways. We
outdo the most sanctimonious of Victorian
clergymen.

That passage is a direct hit on me.

The consequences of this imperialistic attitude can
be most destructive. We begin to be conscious of our
own power as helpers. We perceive our relationships
with a particular family as crucial. We find ourselves
taking the pre-Copernican position. We see social
work, medicine or nursing at the absolute centre of
the social universe whereas, more truly, professional
helping is always peripheral to the main caring
energy.

Worse still, voluntary caring can be seen as inferior
or merely supplementary to professional helping.
Consider this passage from a report on voluntary
workers in the social services.

It is not surprising that members of a profession
whose boundaries have still to be defined, and
which has grown up so rapidly and so recently,
should still find it difficult to reconcile their view
of themselves, as people trained to undertake
skilled work and to deal with complex problems,
with the idea that volunteers can help them in their
work.[13]

The number of times I have heard a neighbour say of
a client 'I should like to have helped but I'm not
qualified.'

When you measure the gigantic forces of caring for
one another existing within the community,
professionalized helping emerges as a grain of sand on

a large beach. To whom would you go in distress? Who helped you last when you needed it? Social work in particular has failed to see the vital role of friends, relatives and neighbours. Bill Jordan writes[14] 'Because social work was originally established to help such people as individuals, and to try to raise them up to an "acceptable" pattern of behaviour, it sees others who share their difficulties as a threat, because they are likely to drag down again those who are being helped.'

Helping should place more general stress on assisting the community's own helping process rather than being dedicated to the direct help of individuals, although both kinds of intervention are required. Widening the spectrum of helping has been handicapped by increasing distance between consumers and professionals.[15] 'The distance between the givers and the receivers of service is increasing daily, particularly so in view of social work's drive toward increased specialisation.'

Helpers and helped have traditionally come from different social backgrounds. The two groups read different newspapers, live on different sides of the rail-track and have quite different educational backgrounds. Many consumer studies illustrate how difficult this makes effective communication.[16, 17, 18] Helper and helped live in parallel universes with just the occasional flash of genuine exchange. The irony is that they live very similar lives, in suffering, ill-health and eventually dying. It is the social clothing which makes contact so difficult.

The last category is structural iatrogenesis where health professions actually undermine the potential of people to deal with their own human weakness, vulnerability and uniqueness in a personal and autonomous way. It paralyses a healthy approach to suffering. It reduces people to the status of passive consumers who are no longer taking any real part in their own treatment and healing.

A year ago I had a personless finger. I had damaged my little finger and as it did not heal up after several weeks I visited the local hospital which prescribed treatment. After several months I received another appointment and stood in a long line awaiting the consultant. He received my case-file and finger simultaneously. In the few moments' examination he did not look up at my face. 'Yes,' he said thoughtfully, 'Your finger does not hurt any more. It is completely healed and I am discharging you.' It did hurt and was not, in my view as its owner, fully healed but I left silently still keeping religiously to my role as passive consumer.

Do you remember the conversations between Kostoglotov, the far from passive consumer, and his doctor Dontsova in *Cancer Ward*?[19]

'You will go home,' Dontsova weighed her words one by one with great emphasis, 'when I consider it necessary to interrupt your treatment. And then you will go temporarily.'

Kostoglotov had been waiting for this moment in the conversation. He couldn't let it go by without a fight. 'Ludmila Afanasyeva! Can't we get away from this tone of voice? You sound like a grown up talking to a child. Why not talk as an adult to an adult? Seriously, when you were on your rounds this morning. . . .'

'Yes, on my rounds this morning' — Dontsova's big face looked quite threatening — 'you made a disgraceful scene. What are you trying to do?

Upset the patients? What are you putting into their heads?'

'What was I trying to do?' He spoke without heat but emphatically, as Dontsova had. He sat up, his back firm against the back of the chair. 'I simply wanted to remind you of my right to dispose of my own life. A man can dispose of his own life, can't he? You agree I have the right?'

Dontsova looked down at his colourless, winding scar and was silent. Kostoglotov developed his point:

'You see, you start from a completely false position. No sooner does a patient come to you than you begin to do all his thinking for him. After that, the thinking's done by your standing orders, your five minute conferences, your programmes, your plan and the honour of your medical department. And once again I become a grain of sand, just like I was in the camp. Once again nothing depends on me.'

I have attended many case conferences, far away from the Soviet Union, which operated on very similar principles of undermining the patient's autonomy. We can gain professional confidence and personal security at our consumer's expense — by taking over the running of his life.

The danger is that we all seek some measure of dependence. We look for someone to trust and lean on.[20]

It is all too easy to become dependent, to push problems on to someone else's plate. Social workers, for instance, are over-committed, carrying out their daily duties and implementing abundant

and complex social legislation. But the more they
do, the more they are expected to do. How horrific
it is to read in newspapers reports about the death
of an elderly person whose body is not discovered
till weeks later. How much more horrific to read
the neighbour's comment, 'It isn't my duty to go
and see if he/she is all right. It's the social
worker's.'

We seem to have invested all powers of initiative
and decision-making in professionalism and
administration. Curiously we create institutions to
deal with problems. The institutions create
dependence on the part of those who work in
them. We start out to help people and end up by
crippling them. As their problems become worse,
so conventional thinking has it that we should
establish yet more institutions — a need which
never gets fulfilled because we then say we can't
afford it.

How can we break that vicious circle? How can
professional and voluntary helping be used to expand
the quantity and the quality of the community's
caring?

As usual Ivan Illich points out some important
directions.[21]

The recovery of autonomous action will depend
not on new specific goals people share, but on their
use of legal and political procedures that permit
individuals and groups to resolve conflicts arising
from their pursuit of different goals. . . . Better
health care will not depend on some new
therapeutic standard, but on the level of
willingness and competence to engage in self-care.

41

The recovery of this power depends on the
recognition of our present delusions.

For me, those delusions in helping mean a stress
on more and more professionalized helping; seeing
our professional contribution as central rather than
peripheral; an increased reliance on social engineering
methods of change. We need to re-examine the whole
notion of helping ourselves and others.

Many consumers require material help and advice
rather than psychotherapy. Their distress is more
closely linked with environmental situations rather
than deep internal longings and dissatisfactions. There
may well be a large gap between what clients 'want'
and what they 'need' but who is to be the judge of
that gap?

There is a widening chasm between what clients
say they want as a service and what professional
helpers are prepared to contribute. Specialization in
problem areas and method develop in ways which
seem to have very little relevance to the resources and
pathology of the community. The Southampton
social work study[22] found a wide difference between
the declared interests of the local authority social
work staff and the measured needs of the community
it serves. We have growing problems of poverty and
social isolation among the elderly but notoriously
little interest among social work students. This gap
may be another consequence of increased social
distance between professionals and consumers.

How can we work to preserve the autonomy of
those we assist? How can we protect our consumers
against the mainly unintended consequences of what
we do? We need pressingly to chart our own
incompetence and drive for power. We can map out

the tensions between wanting to protect and
surround ourselves with warmth and security and
the actual service to the community. What kinds of
basic knowledge and skills ought the various
helpers to have?

Is it actually possible to give help whilst intending
to give it? Can effective help be given by those who
are paid for the sole purpose of giving it? Frequently
the clients are placed in a subordinate and
uncomfortable position. The kind of help received
from friends and relatives feels quite different from
that given by professionals.

I went twice to see a consultant psychiatrist in the
late sixties as a patient. I felt humiliated not by the
consultant but by the process. At the time, it seemed
I had joined the ranks of the mentally ill, the socially
inadequate and the weak. Looking back at the
experience, I see it as enriching. It was the first plain
confession that someone, who was normally regarded
by family, colleagues and clients as robust, also
needed help and solace. But the psychiatrist emerges
as a shadowy figure. Who was he? Did he care about
me as a person? Was I just another student
psychiatric case to him?

I know that I matter to friends and relatives. They
see me as important and usually give help freely and
intimately. Help just flows from them without
apparent ulterior motive or exterior design. I perceive
them as equals and not as superior beings. They are
very much in the same boat as I. At some future
time, they may also need my help.

Professionals can learn to help indirectly through
neighbourhood schemes and new careers projects.[23]
Some helpers are experimenting in providing training
for 'new careers' for ex-offenders and alcoholics as

social service staff. The former prisoner or drug addict can help run a hostel for people with those kinds of difficulties.

As well as helping indirectly, we can persistently place the interests of our customers before those of our own. Too frequently we regard our own self-interest and that of our profession as concomitant with the good of the community. Too frequently and humanly we work out our own personal problems on the clients. Far worse, clients can become a human battleground for interdepartmental squabbles in which all sight of anyone's human needs is obscured.

We can be honest about our failings and incompetence. There are some traditional games which involve putting the blame on 'the high-ups'. A social worker might recommend that a client does not receive some financial grant and returning to him and listening to bitter complaints says 'Don't blame me. It's absolutely nothing to do with me. They make all those decisions up there.'

Very much of helping practice, particularly as professionals, is concerned with insuring the administrative machine against blame and responsibility. There is a tension between the department's overall machinery and responsibility and the individual who works for it. Expediency versus Integrity. I remember my senior officer continually saying 'Cover yourself, David.' He meant I had to be insured against any eventuality. No matter what happened to whom or by what means, my hands were clean because I had been through all the correct administrative motions. Pontius Pilate.

Honesty and explicitness are good bedfellows. If we are translucent in our work with people, they can exercise a good deal of control over what

direction the relationship takes. Translucency about
methods as well as aims. We can tell our consumers
about the way we do our work as well as its
directions. We can tell them what we consider
'realistic' and how that differs from their perception.

There is room for a greater teaching/learning
element in ordinary helping. If we take seriously the
'client as colleague' philosophy it follows that we
teach some of the interviewing methods and casework
principles, health care and skills as they seem relevant
to the client. There is a great potential in our practice
for imparting skills and knowledge about human
growth and development for example. Health visitors
have given a good lead in this. We could extend that
fine Christian Aid slogan 'Give a man a fish, feed him
for a day. Teach him to fish, feed him for life.'

But the teaching is not just one way. When
supervising, the question I ask most often of students
in fieldwork practice is 'What did your clients teach
you during the last week?' There is a real sense in
which good advice to a young social worker might
be — go to your practice, and your clients will teach
you all there is to know.

D. H. Lawrence had a phrase 'the greed of giving'
and this is common amongst helpers. We often receive
very badly. We prefer to be giving out rather than
taking in but this is often what the consumer needs
most. If placed in a position as the eternal recipient
his whole ego can be undermined. He also needs the
possibility to genuinely donate something of value to
both the relationship and society.

For me the hardest element of all in the interviews
with the psychiatrist was that it was a situation of
simply receiving. There seemed no way in which I
could give to the relationship. I could not learn about

him as an individual or give him insights or feelings
that could be anything but a liability or burden. That
is how it felt.

We have to wrestle with our personal desire to have
things *our* way. We have to learn a genuine respect,
based on compassion rather than pity, for our clients
no matter how dirty, disorganized, aggressive or
rejecting they may seem. Out of this respect can flow
good helping; help for us as well as them.

We have to lay limits to our interference in the
lives of others. As my Zen teacher puts it:[24]

> By virtue of walking the Way, the childish 'I want',
> the passions or emotions, are transformed. What in
> fact happens is that the energy (strength) loses the
> blind compulsion of a drive and becomes amenable
> to conscious choice. In this lies the virtue of seeing
> clearly and of being able to act in accordance with
> that seeing. This embraces all the truly human
> qualities, such as responsibility, justice,
> consideration, warmth of heart, joy, tolerance,
> compassion, awareness of strength of personality
> and its power and limits. For nobody has the right
> to manipulate anybody or to impress anybody
> with his stronger personality, not even for the
> other's imagined good, for nobody can know what
> that good is. This is courtesy rather than
> callousness, for the other's dignity is thus
> acknowledged, or the dignity of his grief is
> respected. If and when he is ready, the other will
> of himself reach out for consolation and feel free
> to ask for a hand to point out the way.

4 Compassion

> If only
> I could throw away
> the urge
> to trace my patterns
> in your heart
> I could really see you.

When Bankei held his seclusion weeks of
meditation, pupils from many parts of Japan came
to attend. During one of these gatherings a pupil
was caught stealing. The matter was reported to
Bankei with the request that the pupil be expelled.
Bankei ignored the case.

Later the pupil was caught in a similar act, and
again Bankei disregarded the matter. This angered
the other pupils, who drew up a petition asking for
the dismissal of the thief, stating that otherwise
they would leave in a body.

When Bankei had read the petition he called
everyone before him. 'You are wise brothers,' he
told them. 'You know what is right and what is
not right. You may go somewhere else to study if
you wish, but this poor brother does not even
know right from wrong. Who will teach him if I do
not? I am going to keep him here even if all the
rest of you leave.'

A torrent of tears cleansed the face of the

brother who had stolen. All desire to steal had
vanished.[1]

The story of Bankei is full of compassion which is
at the core of helping. He was generous both to the
thief and to the self-righteous pupils. He saw clearly
the need of the petitioners to look at their own
self-righteousness and the consequences of protecting
property. He taught an enlightening lesson about the
dangers of passing judgments similar to those lessons
of Christ. Who can cast the first stone? Who is better
than another?

Compassion is an unpopular word nowadays. It
points towards commitment, involvement, caring,
love and generosity of heart. These are directions
closely related to feeling and sentiment, sources of
considerable embarassment for twentieth-century
man. It is less dangerous to be cool than passionate
in contemporary society. However, compassion lies
at the heart of all helping; without it relationships
between people are like dry leaves in the wind.

Openness, intimacy and sensitivity are the herbs of
compassion. Those qualities are concerned with
seeing deeply and directly into the other person and
feeling his needs and wants. That has nothing to do
with verbal diarrhoea. Being compassionate does not
mean giving people the everlasting benefit of your
advice, telling them the intimate details of your nasal
operation or leg wound. Genuine caring is much less
conspicuous and unself-conscious.

The beginning of compassion both to oneself and
to others is in decreasing the number of judgments. I
begin to see what is there without continuously
labelling the events with the colours of my
judgments and values. I stop punishing myself for

falling short of standards which I erected. I see the
way someone behaves and do not feel that it is either
bad or good. That desire had melted away by feelings
of respect for the other's independence. He or she is
not there anyway to suit or satisfy my view of the
world.

'I know exactly how you feel' must be mistaken
however good the intent of the speaker. How can it
be possible to make any kind of accurate analogy,
experiential or otherwise, between two persons'
feelings, even about an apparently similar happening?
When you tell me about the death of a friend, it is
most probable that it is my pain I feel about the
death of someone close to me. I cannot tell whether
what moves inside my heart is similar to that which
moves inside yours. I can share it but must be careful
not to drown your grief and sorrow with my own.

Compassion means giving people room; opening
doors rather than closing them; asking questions
rather than giving answers. It means becoming
sensitively aware of another person's situation and
feelings. It means listening with your whole being and
giving, if you can, what is relevant and appropriate
to the relationship without self-consciously measuring
what that is. 'I went away warmed by his quiet
attention to my words, and by his ability to imply
with a smile or gesture, the sharing of a common
humanity.'[2]

Compassion is the process of deep contact with
the primordial source of love. It is the direct
communication from the innermost recesses of one's
existence.

Compassion has nothing to do with achievement at
all. It is spacious and very generous. When a person

develops real compassion, he is uncertain whether
he is being generous to others or to himself because
compassion is environmental generosity, without
direction, without 'for me' and without 'for them'.
It is filled with joy, spontaneously existing joy,
constant joy in the sense of trust, in the sense
that joy contains tremendous wealth, richness.[3]

The highest level of compassion is without any
purpose or intent. It seeks neither the good of others
nor its own good. It lies in being good not 'doing
good'. There is simply living without design or
conscious reflection. It embodies the fostering of
love.

Zen Buddhists use the term Karuna to describe a
process rather than a quality in particular people.
Suzuki wrote:[4]

When Prajna [wisdom] is attained, we have an
insight into the fundamental significance of life
and the world, and cease to worry about
individual interests and sufferings. Karuna is free
to work its way, which means that love,
unobstructed by its selfish encumbrances, is able
to spread itself over all things.

At this highest level, Karuna does not attach itself
to the intricacies of suffering or to individual human
situations. It is involved with the salvation of all living
things. It spreads out the map of enlightenment for
all who care to look.

That is the way of the Buddhas. I am very much
concerned with those individuals who live around me.
I continually 'judge' myself as being inadequate when
judged against all sorts of standards in my head. Most

of the energy in my helping comes from feelings of
pity felt towards others. Pity is one part arrogance
and one part sympathy. Unlike compassion it sees
others as unequal, inferior.

Its intent is a mission to help others who are
perceived as 'less adequate'. The echoes of smugness
and complacency can drown the genuine giving and
hinder people. Such a mixture is all that is possible at
present for me. I travel on a pathway of meditation
and acceptance, both of myself and others, which
may uncover less selfish, striving effort.

Travelling along this pathway does not mean the
development of quietism, withdrawal from the world
or acquiescence in suffering and cruelty. It actually
means a much firmer entry into everyday life — the
hoeing of the garden and the troubles and joys of
both family and friends. Instead of becoming a social
anaesthetic, meditation involves a greater immersion
in the simple process of living.

For many, such voyages are associated with the
labels of 'self-indulgence' or even of 'psychological
masturbation'. This attitude reveals a definite split
between the worlds of service to fellow man and
inner reflection. It sees the two as quite separate. In
Zen existence is an inseparable whole, an overall
unity, in which we embrace and are also embraced by
the whole universe. That view is opposed to a
withdrawal from the world. '. . . it follows that we
cannot attain genuine peace of mind merely by
seeking our own salvation while remaining indifferent
to the welfare of others.'[5]

Genuine self-discovery cannot cut itself off from
the cries of those who suffer because of famine and
physical pain. The traveller hears those cries and sees
the suffering. Those experiences are part of

journeying towards enlightenment. He helps where he can and experiences pain and alienation. His own greed and selfishness contribute in no small way to the suffering of the world.

Generosity is an important component of compassion. But giving has many pit-falls to trap the unwary and unsighted. It can effectively help inflate the ego. In the helping process it can become a peculiar form of parsimony. It deprives others. Helpers lust to give in a showering of tangible and verbal presents like the worst form of Santa Claus. Each gift re-affirms the inferiority of the recipient. Each gift becomes an indication of the pity felt by the giver. 'I am sorry for you. . . .'

In the Greek Street community for homeless women I lived next door to Joanna who had been ten years in a psychiatric hospital diagnosed as 'acute schizophrenic'. She slept in the large linen-room and cursed me loudly through the thin cardboard wall for continuously sexually interfering with her. I was sorry for Joanna and tried very hard to communicate. The response was a long whispered incoherent discourse with certain words like 'laser beams' and 'rape' repeated over and over again. Several times each night I would wake up because she was banging on the wall and screaming 'Rape, rape . . .' I tried to help her but nothing seemed to work.

One weekend I was writing a pamphlet, 'Women without Homes', for Christian Action which had to be finished by the Monday. I was very tired and depressed. Each time I used the typewriter Joanna would scream. I knew that she felt my typewriter was a laser machine. I tried pleading, cajoling, knocking on the wall and cursing to no avail.

Finally, in desperation I looked out my earlier

pamphlet and wrote her a note.

Dear Joanna,
I am trying to write another pamphlet like
'Homeless in London' which I enclose. It has to
be finished this weekend. Please help me by
remaining silent.

I shoved the pamphlet and note under her door and
went back to my room. After an hour or so, I heard a
shuffling and the pamphlet was returned under the
door. Inside was a scrawled note. 'David, I enjoyed
the pamphlet. Please continue.' I typed on into the
night and there were no sounds. She was helping me.
For the first time a social worker needed help from
her.

People who seek or are seen as requiring assistance
frequently need also a way to give something worth
while.

It is well known that the poor are more willing to
give than the rich. Nevertheless, poverty beyond a
certain point may make it impossible to give, and
is so degrading, not only because of the suffering it
causes directly, but because of the fact that it
deprives the poor of the joy of giving.[6]

I have known families in severe poverty, without
beds, real furniture or proper food supplies,
persistently defined and treated as mendicants and
suppliants. Help came to them as handouts in a truly
feudal context with little sense of their own dignity
or worth. Sometimes the 'help' would come and
thinly disguise a strong contempt expressly seeing
them as 'malingerers' or 'wasters'. Those families had

either become bitter or had learned thoroughly a whole ritual unctiousness, to gain benefits which ought, anyway, to have been theirs by right.

Such giving often comes with strings attached. 'I will give you this if. . . .' The if can mean 'improve your behaviour, take better care of your children, pay your rent more regularly, clean yourself up. . . .' Rarely are the implicit strings and conditions and resulting sanctions spelled out to the recipient. The Helping Game is much more complex and misty than that. Sanctions may mean a withdrawal of promised aid or support; a recommendation for eviction or taking the children into care; or simply and cosmologically 'I will not care for you any more.'

Genuine compassion cannot be glued together so easily with ulterior motives particularly those which remain concealed. I may consider that life would be better for you if you were to bathe more frequently, spoke properly or managed your money more efficiently. I cannot *know* that that is the case. Helping is frequently embroidered with emotional blackmail of all kinds. Sometimes the blackmail has to do with the functions of an agency desiring certain ends and certain kinds of behaviour; sometimes to do with the personal needs of the helping agent. There is a great difference between spelling out what you think might be the consequences of certain proposed actions by the client and leaning heavily on him to behave in a certain way.

The nature of compassion is to widen choices rather than narrow them. Getting my own way as helper is not the object of the process at all. My notion of widening the options may not co-incide with that of the client's view. That divergence should be the beginning of a continuing and important discussion between us. I have to be careful in the way I use power that I do not play the tune whilst he foots the bill.

Giving can be much more for the benefit of the giver than for the good of the recipient. Givers can become obsessed with the process of 'doing good to people'. It can become an important drive and even a sickness in which they urgently need the continuing contact with recipients to give added meaning to their lives. Helping becomes a drug. This can hide an aching emptiness and real good cannot come easily from such restless energy.

We have continually to examine the source of our caring energy. It can come from many sources. Herschel Prins argues that[7] it can come from curiosity, creativity, as well as from unconscious needs to punish, to control others, to solve one's own problems.

It is hard to achieve some fine balance between reaching out and self-exploration. I have heard social workers and doctors sob in groups that they were thoroughly miserable and unloved but 'I don't have time for myself. The clients are much worse off than me and much more important.' These people can be left feeling empty and desperate.

There are many people who spend all their time giving aid to the needy and joining movements for the betterment of society. To be sure, this ought not to be discounted. But their root anxiety, growing out of their false view of themselves and the universe, goes unrelieved, gnawing at their hearts and robbing them of a rich and joyous life. Those who sponsor and engage in such social betterment activities look upon themselves,

consciously or unconsciously, as morally superior
and so never bother to purge their minds of greed,
anger and delusive thinking. But the time comes
when, having grown exhausted from all their
restless activity, they can no longer conceal from
themselves their basic anxieties about life and
death. Then they seriously begin to question why
life has not more meaning and zest. Now for the
first time they wonder whether instead of trying
to save others they ought not to save themselves
first.[8]

They have not begun the search for a substantial
source of nutrition. All their energy and wandering
empties them. They can find no genuine satisfaction
in helping others because it comes from a desperate
need to escape feelings of isolation and loss. I came
into social work primarily because I felt it was the
only way to find deep and satisfactory human
relationships to ease my own desperate sense of
isolation. My true growth began in experiencing the
sense of isolation rather than in giving to others.
Superiority and self-righteousness are closely
interrelated to each other and moral imperialism. 'I
feel better than you. I feel warm and good about what
I am able to do for the socially isolated and
inadequate.' When we look at the sheer chaos and
misery of our own lives, it makes self-righteousness
seem even more empty and insubstantial.
We need to protect ourselves and others from the
consequences of good intentions even more than
from those of the destructive. When good intentions
are entangled with feelings of moral superiority it
can be twice as dangerous. This mixture can encourage
the recipient to feel worthless and third-rate; seeing

us as 'good' and himself as 'bad'. It is so much harder
to struggle against the pressing attentions of someone
who is intent on undermining you by doing good.

I got very upset at a Quaker Meeting and after
seventeen years of membership never went back. I
felt there had been a good deal of dishonesty and
repressed emotion at a time which called for
emotional expression and authenticity. That was my
crude and angry judgment and on the way to the car
park after the meeting I felt violent with passion. An
elderly Quakeress pulled at my arm.

'Why are you so depressed, David?'

'I'm not depressed. Not at all. I am feeling
absolutely bloody furious with you all.'

'Come and have coffee with me and talk it over.
You'll soon feel better.'

'I do not particularly want to feel better. Thank
you for the offer. I will have coffee with you some
other time.'

'Come and have coffee with me. It is very
unchristian of you to refuse.'

Unchristian or not, I walked off without looking back
and was much too angry to be affected by the final
twist of guilt until later.

Clearly it was important that I had coffee with her
— to her rather than me. I felt she wanted to suck me
in. She was wanting to pour sugared cream over all
my emotions. The offer seemed to have nothing to
do with me and the way I was feeling at that time.

I don't see compassion as necessarily 'making
people feel better'. It is a much more robust process
than this. It does not involve simply being good or
pleasant to people. Saying the right or socially
acceptable thing is not usually being compassionate.
Being nice is a simple ongoing social device to avoid

undue disturbance and pain. Compassion accepts the risks and ignores those dangers.

> Thus the marriage counsellor tells us, the husband should 'understand' his wife and be helpful. He should comment favourably on her new dress, and on a tasty dish. She, in turn, should understand when he comes home tired and disgruntled, she should listen attentively when he talks about his business troubles, should not be angry but understanding when he forgets her birthday. All this kind of relationship amounts to is the well-oiled relationship between two persons who remain strangers all their lives, who never arrive at a 'central relationship', but who treat each other with courtesy and who attempt to make each other feel better.[9]

Without wishing to be quite as scathing as Fromm, the example illustrates form rather than content. Behaving as if you did care may sometimes flower into genuine love. But avoiding trouble, being courteous and patient when it does not spring from your inner being may hinder personal growth. Sadly much helping is aimed at the lubrication of relationships rather than experiencing the situation of lack of caring. Understandably, expediency dominates thinking about help in many settings. 'How can I/we achieve some element of personal comfort?' I see nothing wrong in that.

Real compassion is often uncomfortable and disturbing. It enlightens rather than lubricates. It has few intentions and works in an unflaunting and unself-conscious way.

Highest good is like water. Because water excels
in benefiting the myriad creatures without
contending with them and settles where none
would like to be, it comes close to the Way.[10]

Compassion is the complete reflection of overall
harmony. It contains, as Fromm pointed out in
writing of love, the ingredients of care, responsibility,
respect and knowledge.[11] It is vital to feel caring for
others; to feel concern as to what may be or is
happening to them although this does not necessarily
involve personal affection.

Responsibility means that you are sensitive to
what is being said and done. There is a direct
sensitivity to the consequences of activities and words
going on both within and without the relationship.
Your own intervention is seen as a contributing
factor to the whole process. You have a partial
responsibility for all that happens.

Respect is seeing the Buddha nature in the other
person. It means perceiving the superficiality of
positions of moral superiority. The other person is as
good as you. However untidy, unhygienic, poor,
illiterate and bloody-minded he may seem, he is
worthy of your respect. He also has autonomy and
purpose. He is another form of nature.

Knowledge is coterminous with caring and not in
opposition to it. If you care about someone or
something, you wish to use all your talents, including
the intellectual, to arrive at contact with and an
understanding of the situation. Knowledge can be
an important ingredient of compassion; a reflection,
in part, of how much you care. It becomes a yeast
for the process rather than another barrier between
you and the consumer. Sometimes the professional

uses knowledge to mystify his patient. He pretends to authoritative statements when there is only an experiential fog.

Compassion is being in tune with oneself, the other person(s) and the whole world. It is goodness at its most intuitive and unreflective. It is a harmony which opens itself and permits the flowing out of love towards others without asking any reward. It avoids using people as tools. It sees them as complete and without a need to be changed.

It achieves a balance between outer and inner worlds until they blend. Blyth reminds us of just how difficult that balance is:

How can we establish a harmony between ourselves and the outside world full of misunderstandings, deceit, violence, and the suffering and death of those we love, when all the while we ourselves are full of that same stupidity, insincerity, cruelty and sloth?[12]

One beginning lies in realizing that we paint the world in the poster colours of our own greed, laziness and cruelty as well as in love and caring. It is all human energy. Those injustices that we see and make us feel so angry begin deep inside ourselves.

Real compassion blooms often. Striving after it is somehow both important and irrelevant. Compassion may be watered by effort but is effortless. Effort is self-conscious; compassion flows quietly and naturally from the nature of being.

A young child has perfect, indiscriminate universal love for all things. As he grows older he makes the mistake of supposing that some things are friendly and others are antagonistic to him.[13]

His fears and continuing judgments ripple out into
stereotypes and systems of inclusion and exclusion
which become cruder and more generalized. His mind
categorizes and is made up about a broader range of
phenomena. He shuts off parts of himself which he
may never fully reach again. They become shrouded
in painful memories. He spends much energy
defending this soreness against those suspected of
wishing to trample over it. Finally he continually
emphasizes his growing consciousness of difference
and separation rather than of closeness and oneness.

> The deepest need of man, then, is the need to
> overcome his separateness, to leave the prison of
> his aloneness.[14]

Leaving that particular prison is to discover both
fear and compassion.

5   Nowness

In meditation practice, the most elusive point of
concentration is nowness. You focus all energy in the
ingoing and outgoing breath. The door swings open
and shut. You strive for that still point of the present
and see it eternally escaping the grasp. Nowness is a
flowing river. You may get your fingers wet but the
quality of riverness flows through your clutching hands.

The emotions drift in the current. They are logs
and branches which seem to arrive carefully labelled
anger, greed and fear. Each of these has attached to it
a further label saying bad and horrible. What is the
nature of the energy before I label and make my
decisions about value? I struggle to discover but the
river flows ever faster.

Nowness is with us, of us but yet always elusively
evading our grasp. Bringing ourselves into the here and
now sounds deceptively simple but is essentially
very difficult. We divide life into a series of events
and happenings which are seen as big and small. We
mainly live our lives by concentrating on those
events and people seen as large and important. Living
becomes a series of time holes punctuated by
occasional big happenings. Falling in love can mean
that I live suspended between the especial meetings
with my loved one.

Other times and moments — traces of the past and
shadows of the future — crowd into our awareness of

the present moment. Sometimes they are clear; often
rather foggy. Nowness practice does not mean
excluding the past and future but an awareness of the
subservience of both to the present moment.

> The essence of meditation is nowness. Whatever
> one tries to practice, is not aimed at achieving a
> higher state or at following some theory or ideal,
> but simply, without any object or ambition, trying
> to see what is here and now. One has to
> become aware of the present moment. . . ."[1]

Putting purposes and patterns of meaning on cause
and effect, can mean missing the integral freshness
and essential value of each moment by seeing it only
as part of some overall jigsaw puzzle. The gap between
my visions of the ideal world and my judgments of
what is happening to and around me is a source of
great suffering.

> Living in the here and now is behaviour derived
> from the Zen experience. Guilt and anxiety are
> children of the past and future. To the extent
> that a person dwells upon the should-have-been or
> might-be of life at the expense of living life in the
> reality of the present, he suffers.[2]

I continually fall short of those standards which I
set myself in contrasting the present situation with
the might-have-been. The here and now is an
important discipline in helping clarify this continuous
friction and punishment. It is the difference between
asking myself 'How ought I to feel?' and 'How do I
feel?'

Now is the only time when we can actually do

anything. I can be guilty about the past, apprehensive
about the future but only in the present can I act.
The ability to be in the present moment is a major
component of mental wellness.³ We commonly
admire certain people as having 'presence' and usually
mean, in part, that they seem to be rooted, to
communicate a sense of dignity in the now.

To what extent can we bring our perceptions and
energies into what is happening all around us and
when that is happening? How much of our energy
seeps away into anxiety and apprehension? The
ability to exclude irrelevant worries and anxieties
about past experiences and future happenings is of
great worth. Many present perceptions are so intensely
coloured by past experience that I can hardly see a
particular person at all. Frequently I observe them
through the superimposed shadows and reflections of
significant people and events in my life.

I had recently taken to avoiding a certain student
in the coffee room. I feel that she is bitter and angry
in her dealings with me. Each time we meet I bring
this belief and memory. I am hurt and respond angrily
and dogmatically although I feel near to tears. My
anger seems to feed her bitterness.

I hardly see her. She becomes a walking symbol for
the thousands of times that people seemed unkind
and unjust. I lash out in the fog and punish myself for
being 'unreasonable' and 'unfair'. It is hard to tell
her what I see happening (which I have now done)
and to hear her own view. This stinking, rotting flesh
of anger and bitterness cannot be anything to do
with me. I will close my eyes and ears until it goes
away.

Frequently it is difficult for me even to hear certain
people. They talk on particularly painful wavelengths

so I turn down the emotional sound. They penetrate the superficiality of certain images I am trying to broadcast. Often I have so much radio static and personal commercials, such an unquiet mind, that their words and feelings are hardly audible. My attention becomes distracted by personal problems or by what children are doing outside the window or in simply being bored by a client's words.

The clients are not there to provide a continuing kaleidoscope of amusement, curiosity and interest for my benefit. They are there to receive some help. Nevertheless I may be communicating my boredom non-verbally. I have told several clients about my boredom with their conversation, especially in group situations.

The responsibility for my boredom is mainly mine. It is always hard to accept responsibility for the unpleasant instead of blaming it onto others. 'I am bored' rather than 'I find you boring.' The first takes some responsibility, albeit silently, whilst the second blames the other person outright. One client was quite relieved when informed. 'I'm glad you told me I was boring you. I was beginning to believe you just weren't human.'

Good listening has an enormous quality of nowness. The listener has made no prior decisions or laid down any precious structure of his own in relation to the speaker. As Carl Rogers wrote:

To me it appears that only as he [counsellor] is completely willing that any outcome, any direction, may be chosen — only then does he realize the vital strength of the capacity and potentiality of the individual for constructive action. It is as he is willing for death to be the choice, that a healthy normality is chosen. The more completely he acts upon his central hypothesis, the more convincing is the evidence that the hypothesis is correct.[4]

This listening is much more than an absence of sound from the listener in the same way that peace is more than a mere absence of war. Chögyam Trungpa identifies three kinds of listening:

In one case, one's mind is wandering so much that there's no room at all for anything that's being said. One is just there physically. This type is said to be like a pot turned upside down. In another case, one's mind is relating somewhat to what's being said, but basically it is still wandering. The analogy is a pot with a hole in the bottom. Whatever you pour in leaks out underneath. In the third case, the listener's mind contains aggression, jealousy, destruction of all kinds. One has mixed feelings about what is being said and cannot really understand it. The pot is not turned upside down, it doesn't have a hole in the bottom, but it has not been cleaned properly. It has poison in it.[5]

Many of the helping questions contain assumptions as to what the answer will be. As Andy Warhol once said to a TV interviewer — 'Tell me clearly what answers you require and I shall repeat them after you. . . .' Questioning and listening which does not structure the answers, except minimally, is a great art.

I was writing a book with a friend who was very physically handicapped. Anne had been a Beauty Queen until paralysed in a car accident. I asked her very carefully what it was like to be handicapped.

'Funny' was her reply.

'But you can't mean funny . . .'

'Yes I do — when I was a little girl, I used to dream about being a fairy princess who was waited on hand and foot. And it came true.'

'But there must be pain and disadvantages.'

'Of course. You see if I had not been in the car accident, life would have been very different but not necessarily better. This way I was forced to explore myself, to meditate. I have become a strong person.'

I was not listening to Anne. She was trying to tell me something quite opposed to my conceptions of physically handicapped people. She was telling me something outside my range of expected answers. She was asking me to unlearn — always very painful.

Helpful listening is simply listening. It is a form of meditation wherein the speaker becomes the object of the concentration rather than the breathing or a mantra. The focus of the helper's concentration is the sound of the speaker's voice and the possible meanings of his words.

Nowness closes no doors. It involves an openness which throws away fears and expectations. It opens itself to risks, to new learning, experiences and interpretations. It declares 'I am ready to see you in a fresh way. I wish to put no boundaries on what you might say or do.'

Maslow writes:

One finds what is right for oneself by listening carefully and Taoistically to one's inner voices, by listening in order to let oneself be moulded, guided, directed. The good psychotherapist helps his patient in the same way — by helping the patient hear his drowned-out inner voices, the weak commands of his own nature on the Spinozistic principle that true freedom consists of accepting and loving the inevitable, the nature of reality.

Similarly one finds out what is right to do with the world by the same kind of listening to its nature and voices, by being sensitive to its requiredness and suggestions, by hushing so that its voices may be heard; by being receptive, non-interfering, non-demanding and letting be.[6]

I felt really in harmony with a man whose wife and family had just left him. His physical health had been deteriorating for several years, reducing his mobility and enjoyment of life considerably. Black depression shrouded him. He had tried to take his life several times. He talked to me at some length about suicide. One question which was repeatedly and pressingly asked was 'Can you see any reason for me to go on living?'

I evaded an answer. I dodged through every psychotherapeutic bush. 'How can I know the answer to that? You have to find your own reason?' My nowness was that I could see every reason for his wish to die but social workers were 'not supposed to tell people that. It might prove destructive.'

This man wanted a genuine answer from me. I thought deeply about his whole life — the depression, poverty, his failing health and the loss of family. Finally I replied 'I can see no reason to go on living in your case. I can see clear reasons for wishing to die.'

I felt afraid. It seemed an enormous risk to say that to him. What kind of responsibility would I have if he finally killed himself? How would I feel?

How is he to respond to my answer? My mind raced off into the future etching complex mental patterns. Months afterwards, when the depression had largely disappeared, he told me that my answer had been helpful. At a time when it seemed everyone was simply giving an unthinking response of pity and sympathy, he had urgently needed an honest answer to that important question.

Years later, I was working as a voluntary helper in an Islington nursery. It was lunchtime and the children were having a cooked meal placed on their small tables. As the meal was served, the children began to sing spontaneously. Soon all the children, West Indian and English, were singing happily. The assistant in charge said kindly but firmly, 'You can sing after lunch children but not now. All your dinners will get cold and uneatable.' They ceased to sing.

Half an hour later, the same assistant began to sing children's songs with the nursery group. She sang solo. The moment for the children had passed. Their attention had moved on to playing with bricks and dolls. She turned to me saying 'Aren't children contrary? They never do what you want them to do.' Uncharacteristically, I remained silent. Those small children, all under five, were thoroughly immersed in the here and now. They had wanted to sing when, to adults, it had seemed inconvenient. Half an hour later that desire had vanished completely.

I received another lesson from a child in Luton. I found myself walking slowly alongside a mother and small child. It was a fine, crisp, wintry morning and near by was a stretch of green patterned with snowdrops. The small child's eyes widened in excitement and she tried to halt her mother. 'Look,

look Mummy, see those lovely flowers.' I stopped and with her tuition saw them but Mum was driven on and down through the weight of the shopping bags and her fear of missing the bus. The child, dragged protestingly along by the mother, boarded the bus a few minutes later. Neither had time to enjoy the snowdrops.

The child's art in immersing himself in present time is difficult for adults to follow. I find myself frequently watching myself watching the children looking at snowdrops in a way which separates me from the outside world. I also find myself watching myself trying to help people.

One of the most difficult skills in group work is that of simply staying with the group members. Your task as leader is to follow the energy of the group and avoid putting your own interpretative patterns and expectations on them. Sitting quietly watching someone work on their personal problems, my mind is buzzing with analogies to past experiences. 'Doesn't she seem just like. . . . I wonder whether she had a poor relationship with her brother and that that influences the way she. . . .'

Nowness means the ability to throw away those intellectualizations when the client goes off in an unexpected direction. How often have I compelled some poor client to come back from some pathway of exploration simply because I was holding firmly to my view of what he *ought* to be doing? I use my power to make what I believe to be true, probably to the detriment of the client.

Helping is a market place for those who want to be in any other time and place except the present one. Pascal puts it precisely:

We never remain in the present. We anticipate the
future as being too slow to come, as if to hasten its
progress; or we recall the past in order to hold it
back as being too quick to go: we are so rash as to
stray into times which are not ours, and do not
think about the only one which belongs to us: so
futile as to think of those which no longer are,
and to let slip unreflecting the only one which
subsists. The truth is that the present commonly
wounds us.[7]

It wounds us primarily because of our yearnings
for different times and places. We crave better
professional status, more money, less heavy caseloads.
Our clients crave more money, better houses in an
improved environment. Resources are irresponsibly
distributed because of the successful greed of the
many. Our lives become a series of loosely linked
'if only' experiences. 'If only I had time to do that . . .
If only I had the money to buy that. . . .' Such wishes
serve mainly to inflate our egos.

When visiting a residential establishment, fieldwork
setting or voluntary society, I commonly ask what
people are doing. How do they spend their day, their
working week? Seldom do I receive an answer which
relates directly to the question. Usually the question
evokes a whole patchwork of dreams and visions
covering deep frustrations and disappointments.

People find it difficult to say what they are doing
at present. They describe what might be happening in
a few months' or years' time. Residential homes
particularly weave a web of fantasies around their
casual visitors. Present activity seems unbearable
because it falls so far short of the visions which the
social worker needs.

During the early months of our government-sponsored research programme into young homelessness, we went through a period of great difficulty. We were interviewing homeless newcomers to central London who persistently gave us inaccurate information. We would ask questions and later learn that many of the answers were fantasies or fabrications. We had expected to spend a great deal of time verifying data but not as much as now seemed required.

I was troubled. It almost seemed that these young people were deliberately frustrating my cherished research programme. We were continually falling over this log of inaccuracy. Then it very slowly dawned that the log which kept tripping us up was of great importance. Why not spend much more time researching the log — examining the kinds of lies and distortions given in interviews — rather than cursing its very existence?

In another research study, we were looking at the problems of homeless families in St. Albans. This meant studying in some detail the functioning of the social services office in that city. We were asking questions like — what was happening to homeless families? What was the style of social work intervention into the problem?

It seemed to us that although there had been a great deal of social work concern and discussion on homelessness in the city, this had resulted in little effective action. One reason given was that social workers felt 'paralysed with depression'. Yet another had a relationship to nowness. Those social workers could see the enormity of the housing problems, the despair of the homeless, and were unable to distinguish between things they could do something

about now and those they simply could do nothing
practical about.

Lack of energy in our present activity is a barrier
to effective change not an aid. One important
prerequisite to change is an acute sensitivity to what
is happening now — however painful that is. If I
truly see what shapes events, the nature of present
disappointments and functioning and accept that
now, then change can begin to take place.[8]

In Western society, we are constantly encouraged
to take our minds away from the present. We are
afraid of boredom. We learn to occupy ourselves
desperately; to do several things simultaneously. We
feel best when busy. Our minds split off in different
directions. We watch ourselves with wrapped
concentration. Our conversation is carefully edited
before it goes out onto the air. It is screened for
social acceptability. 'How will what I say influence
the way others see me?' Such activity is more
concerned with becoming somebody rather than
being someone. We learn to package ourselves, to
protect certain kinds of images rather than simply
to be.

> Swallowing a long
> kebab
> of roles,
> actions
> and thoughts
> only temporarily
> fills
> my hollowness.

Our actions and the events in our lives are seen in
the context of some overall personal plan which goes

'right' or 'wrong'. We do things to achieve status, love or power. We learn to manipulate others and to minimize the social costs of various actions by not taking responsibility for them. Most of our activity becomes an integral part of this life-plan. Life becomes like the numbered dots which children connect up with a pencil and turn out to be the shapes of donkeys or camels.

The shapes we draw are ego shapes. They link our actions and those of others to a conception of image and ego. Our perception of both ego and role provide us with some insurance and security in a world where there seems much risk. We insure against surprises by writing scripts and stories into our lives. We offer explanations of ourselves. We draw patterns of consistency around others and then get angry when they step out of the shape. R.H. Blyth puts this process firmly in its place:

> we are only apparently a unity, a stream of innumerable selves following one another like a series of cinematographic pictures, so quickly that they seem one continuous whole.[9]

This illusion of shape, solidity and continuity is what we call ego. Nowness lies in the absence of the bubble of separation between watcher and watched; a lack of awareness of self. Nowness is the essential direct experience; the unity between helper and helped.

The Buddha told a parable in a sutra:

> A man travelling across a field encountered a tiger after him. Coming to a precipice, he caught hold of the root of a wild vine and swung himself down over the edge. The tiger sniffed at him from above.

Trembling, the man looked down to where, far
below, another tiger was waiting to eat him. Only
the vine sustained him.

Two mice, one white and one black, little by
little started to gnaw away the vine. The man saw
a lucious strawberry near him. Grasping the vine
with one hand, he plucked the strawberry with
the other. How sweet it tasted!'[10]

What magnificent nowness!
Basho, the great Japanese poet, gave this advice:

Go to the pine if you want to learn about the
pine, or to the bamboo. And in doing so, you must
leave your subjective pre-occupation with yourself.
Otherwise you impose yourself on the object and
do not learn. Your poetry issues of its own accord
when you and the object have become one — when
you have plunged deep enough into the object to
see something like a hidden glimmering there.
However well phrased your poetry may be, if your
feeling is not natural — if the object and yourself
are separate — then your poetry is not true poetry
but merely your subjective counterfeit.[11]

A few years ago, I attended a Westernized Zen
sesshin — three days of intense meditation. We went
to bed at midnight each day, in a remote Sussex
manor house, and awoke to the sound of the gong
at 5.45 am. The very long day was spent working in
the garden, walking in meditation or sitting opposite
another student, both of you wrestling with a koan.
Each person received a koan from the Master. Mine
was 'What are you?'

I tried to hold the question in my head but it kept

leaking out. It whirled rapidly round and round and was consistently disturbed by other thoughts, like noisy shooting stars, intruding and tumbling in. Literally hours and hours were spent looking into another student's eyes and trying to answer the question 'What am I?' My legs and spine ached throughout the first day and my bottom became quite numb. My body was so painful and stiff that it was difficult to focus on the question at all.

Whatever we did — whether eating, walking or working, we had to hold on firmly to the question. At the beginning of answering, my mind threw up a whole range of attractive rubbishy phrases. I was dizzy with images and symbols of seashores, mountain glaciers, crystals, slowly opening flowers. Then I went through a period of monsters — black cloaks, lurking shadows and pitch blackness. All were in some way part of me but none comprised the whole.

Thoughts about my family and job came flooding in. I tried to keep my aching spine erect. The answers became even more flowery and poetic. They were bright, shallow images, perfumed and too clever by half. 'I am a question echoing in an empty mind.' My mind darkened and the squirrels played out on the large country lawn. I envied them. They had more sense than to try answering such ridiculous questions.

I saw that I was a candle. A small rather unimportant flickering candle. But the next question was 'Who lit the candle?' How could I be both the candle and the one who lights it? My mind squeezed intensely on this curious paradox. Physically my legs and arms were taut; my chin was stiff and set and teeth held painfully together. Quite suddenly the image of a candle which I had been trying to hold on to had vanished.

I looked at myself intently. I was a knot. My whole
body and mind had become tight and taut like a knot.
But who tied the knot? Who was responsible for the
tension and frustration? Of course I knew who lit the
candle and who tied the knot. Nobody had tried
harder than I to solve the problem and loosen the
ropes. It was simply unfair. It was a trick question
and there was actually no solution at all. It was like
catching sunbeams. I remembered being small and
throwing my jacket over sunbeams on the grass.

Now I seemed lost. Everything lost its clarity. Now
I just clenched my fists, first in anger and then in
despair. I answered 'I am a person who cannot
answer the question.' The question rolled around my
head like a noisy ball. It became difficult to
concentrate. I began to convince myself that I did not
have the necessary precision to obtain an answer. My
mind was a fuzz. Perhaps in the next re-incarnation. . .

Outside the wintry afternoon gave way to darkness
and a biting wind. I walked up and down in a very
large, high-ceilinged stables. My stride quickened and
I kicked out at pieces of stick and stones. The
question came over and over again like a pendulum
'What am I? What am I?' The words became a shout
and then a whole scream of anger from a tense face
and mouth. 'What am I? I am a bloody idiot who
does not know what he is. Who cannot answer a
simple question.' My cries got louder and louder.
Rain and wind carried them back to me. This
shuffling, shouting, scruffy figure in the stables
punched at the air. Every muscle was tight. I was
going to burst.

At the very moment of bursting frustration; at the
very height of all the wind, rain and fury, I was aware,

quite softly, that I was actually keeping the answer
at bay. Like an old and discreet friend, he had been
patiently waiting to come in all this time. He came
in and my whole body relaxed and jumped, felt
good and warm. NOW I was now — the answer
was NOW. I am/was/shall be everything which
unfolds and moves, thinks, questions and talks
at that moment in time. It was far more than a
purely intellectual realization — it bathed me with my
goodness, everyone's goodness. Goodness happening
now. I shouted happily 'Now, now, now'. I and the
question had become friends.

This experience has stayed with me even though it
did not last. I tried unwisely to hold on to its
remnants and got sad when the old divisions and
separateness came flooding back into my heart. I
crave for a return to that experience. I want to be
whole again even for a brief moment. That is to
experience the nowness all inside and through me so
that I am not simply watching myself any more.

All around me, children are showing how it is done.
Looking at the snowdrops. They skip with ropes,
whizz about on roller skates; drink orange pop and
eat ice-creams whilst I watch me watching them and
experience pain.

6 Taoistic change

If you changed
I would probably
like you.
So
why don't you
take the risk?

There is an increasing awareness that much of Western
thought is alienated from natural processes and living
experiences. It has only been quite recently, largely
through the influence of ecology and the pollution
question, that we have been reminded that we are
part of nature. We had learned to consider ourselves
as entirely external to the world. The world
surrounded us but somehow did not extend into us.

Our whole pattern of living emphasizes
separateness, privacy, selfness, distinctions and
ownership. Our language is saturated with 'I's' and
'mines'.

We try to segregate ourselves from the external,
and this creates a kind of bubble in us which
consists of nothing but air and water, or in this
case, fear and reflection of the external thing. So
this huge bubble prevents any fresh air from
coming in, and that is 'I' — the Ego.[1]

This ego is hard and masculine. It is determined to
penetrate rather than to be penetrated. It is the
energy of chopping wood rather than that of the
surfer. It wrestles with life rather than swimming
with it. The central qualities of its nature are
organizing and shaping rather than pliancy and
suppleness. Charles Reich describes twentieth-century
Western consciousness as 'convinced that man's
needs are best met by trying to dominate experience
rather than being subject to experience.' It reflects
the insistence that ' "real" experience is that which
is dominated, not that which comes to the individual
who is unguarded and open. . . .'[2]

A letter to *New Society* illustrates this process. The
writer is describing the development of a playground
in Brighton.

> When Kempton branch-line closed, the railway
> cuttings became perfect natural playgrounds for
> local children who tunnelled camps into the chalk
> and built houses and swings in the trees.
> Undisturbed by the traffic they slid down the
> banks on tin trays or simply flopped about in the
> long grass.
>   Then Brighton council had the great idea of
> using the railway cutting land to create a much
> needed children's play park. The bulldozers were
> moved in, all the bushes and trees were chopped
> down leaving acres of barren chalk which is now
> being covered with imaginative tarmac. The entire
> area is at present fenced off with chain-link fencing
> littered up by 'keep out' notices. At no point did
> the council consult the experts — the children of
> Brighton. They might perhaps have heeded the
> child who remarked 'seems a bit daft to me — all

them bulldozers — that knocking down our camp
and tree house just to build a soppy old park —
where we gonna *play* now?'[3]

Helpers may not only define the world as outside
themselves but also succeed in externalizing the
whole process of change. It is others who are
perceived as the objects of likely change; who are
defined as socially inadequate, incomplete or
mentally ill and so need to 'improve' in some way.
Self-discovery within helpers becomes viewed as an
indulgence taking valuable time away from the
manipulation of change in others! The currently
popular term 'catalyst' is ironically and
unintentionally appropriate as it means strictly 'an
agent in an effect produced by a substance that
without undergoing change itself aids a chemical
change in other bodies' *(Oxford English Dictionary)*.

Not only is this ego oblivious to its own
deficiencies but it becomes greedily certain of its
central importance in life. I recall supervising a rather
breathless social work student. She returned from her
second interview with a very deprived family and
exclaimed 'You wouldn't believe all the changes
which have taken place since my first visit. Everyone
seems to have taken my advice. Little Bob has gone
back to school and Mum has got out of bed at last
and Dad is off to work. . . .' In her mind, her visiting
was at the very centre of the family's situation. Those
people orbitted around her own sphere of influence.
She seemed unaware that the sky is full of similar
suns, stars and planets.

Her arrogance and thoughtlessness finds echoes in
my heart. It is at the basis of much of my motives in
the helping of others. I came into social work in order

to 'change things for the better'. I wanted to
evangelize, to help build a world where people were
much better off and resources were more evenly
shared. I wished to gain power, to influence the lives
of as many people as possible. Initially, I did not see
myself as requiring change at all.

Most of our notions and feelings about change
relate to 'being better' either in ourselves or others.
To me 'better' means being less angry, impatient,
aggressive, unreasonable and unfair. I want to
reject the 'bad' and unruly side of myself; to push
it down deep into the depths. I wish that I did not
judge and punish myself when seen to be falling
short of internalized standards of goodness.

To judge is to stand outside the experiencing and
to ascribe values to it. 'That was a complete waste
of time.' 'I behaved very badly to that person.' We
crave after idealized images. 'The state and
socialisation persuades a child that "life" consists of a
position achieved, and not in a living process.'[4]

I learn to administer advice and wisdom to others
but am unable to apply it to my own life.

> DEAR CLIENT . . .
> Wafting wise words
> across the room
> wishing that I could
> feed myself
> from that same wisdom.

I can find myself a personal hall of mirrors. Each
mirror tells me that I am too tall, fat, short or thin.
The information is entirely contradictory and so I
can dance about trying to satisfy one image whilst
growing further away from others. Such a process

involves the conscious disowning of large areas of self; trying not to think or become too aware of my personal greediness, aggression or egocentricity.

Little is known about the historical beginnings of that school of Chinese philosophy called Taoism. Its founder is said to have been Lao Tzu which is Chinese for old man. If he ever existed, he would have been an older contemporary of Confucius in the sixth century BC. Taoism simply means the school of the Way. Tao stands for something which cannot be named and which exists before the beginning of the world. Its followers see that Heaven and Earth came into being with themselves, and all things are one in unity. 'In this vision all things are relative, all opposites blend, all contrasts are harmonised. The One is Tao. It is the total spontaneity of all things.'[5]

Chang Chung-yuan writes:

In this unity everything breaks through the shell of itself and interfuses with every other thing. Each identifies with every other. The one is many and the many is one. In this realm all selves dissolve into one, and all our selves are selves only to the extent that they disappear into all other selves. Each individual merges into every other individual.[6]

Contrast this situation with the Western experience where we feel powerless and impotent. Our experience continually falls short of our expectation. We feel alienated; distant from one another, overwhelmed by gigantic forces. Rollo May calls this the problem of personal powerlessness in which people feel unable to influence and change others. There is a daily realization, he argues, that 'we cannot influence many people; that we count for little; that the values

to which our parents devoted their lives are to us
insubstantial and worthless. . . .' He feels that a
society which helps its members to feel powerless is
storing up trouble. 'Deeds of violence in our society
are performed largely by those trying to establish their
self-esteem, to defend their self-image, and to
demonstrate that they, too, are significant.'[7] There
is little feeling of harmony here, only a series of
jarring and discordant battles.

Our clients feel even more powerless. They are
poor, handicapped and disaffiliated.[8] They are cut
off from pathways which might give them access to
influencing important political and economic
decisions which affect their daily lives. Some feel
this primarily in psychological ways, that others have
influence over them, that they cannot make friends
and so feel isolated or stigmatized. Another group
experiences it primarily in material terms; that it is
impossible to get adequate accommodation,
employment and educational opportunities. Both
groups feel done to rather than doing.

We are conscious of the effects of material
deprivation but have done very little practical to
counter its depressant and sapping nature. Charles
Reich writes:

> The great mistake of radicals has been to try to
> interest workers in a revolt based primarily on
> material justice. The real deprivation has not been
> in terms of material goods but in terms of a
> deadened mind, a loss of feeling, a life that excludes
> all new experience. This is the true nature of
> contemporary servitude.[9]

Allowing for a few degrees of overstatement, he hits

on a basic truth in relation to helping.

Helping people to become aware of their exploitation is an important process. It is an increased awareness of being exploited or exploiting and joining with others to do something about the whole situation. Paulo Freiro calls this conscientization. This 'refers to the process in which men, not as recipients, but as knowing subjects, achieve a deepening awareness both of the socio-cultural reality which shapes their lives and of their capacity to transform that reality.'[10]

Clients may perceive a variety of helpers as pathways to influence. Social workers can be their advocates for welfare and housing rights; a means for exploring their early life and possibly exorcising uncontrolled demons. Doctors can teach about self-care and health.

Frequently relationships between clients and helpers are grossly unequal in a way which supports hindering and the undermining of autonomy. Genuine communication is frustrated by profuse professional jargon and crude labelling. Helpers use their own status, social position and knowledge to erect barriers rather than to establish genuine harmony and growth.

To the Taoists the notion of harmony was all important. They saw everything as part of the great whole. As their most famous philosopher wrote:

the true nature of wu wei [no mind] is not mere inactivity but perfect action — because it is act without activity. In other words, it is action not carried out independently of Heaven and Earth and in conflict with the dynamics of the whole, but in perfect harmony with the whole.[11]

Those actions came out of the core of being. They were in complete harmony with his authentic nature and the balance of the whole. Occasionally we get this experience in helping others. There are moments when we become unaware of our desire to impress people or even 'to do good' but flow simply from one person to another.

Unfortunately, so much of our helping is self-conscious and self-reflective. Instead of arising simply like a mountain stream from our essential nature, it appears in the ego mist as an object to be strived after and attained. Thomas Merton wrote:

> the more one seeks 'the good' outside oneself as
> something to be acquired, the more one is faced
> with the necessity of discussing, studying,
> understanding, analysing the nature of good. The
> more, therefore, one becomes involved in
> abstractions and in the confusion of divergent
> opinions. The more 'the good' is objectively
> analysed, the more it is treated as something to be
> attained by special virtuous techniques, the less
> real it becomes.[12]

Such a striving pathway takes us perilously close to self-righteousness. We become acutely aware of our own personal goodness in a Phariseeical manner. Continually, we seek first outside ourselves rather than looking inside. Taoists would have to turn away from journeying towards those external ideals and encourage the simply listening to the echoes of our own deep pools. First seek within ourselves.

Change is happening both outside, inside and through us, minute by minute. We die gradually and others are born. R.H. Blyth writes:

The fact is, that we are bound by karma as an
ordinary man is bound by a rock, or by a motor
car that won't go. The sculptor is master of the
rock, the mechanic of the machine, in so far as they
are willingly in accord with the laws of the material
in which they work. . . . We are to live with life
and die with death, not separated from them. The
problem of suffering is insoluble, because we think
of ourselves as apart from pain and death, in
opposition to them. We can be free from change
only by changing with it.[13, 14]

The tragedy of helping is that so often we attempt
to manage social processes. Professionals increasingly
use the language of management — 'motivation' and
'task-oriented interviewing' and 'assessable objectives'.
We see ourselves as being in charge of rather than
working with. Social workers asking me about group-
work training often say 'How can I learn to manage
a small group? How can I organize people in this
particular setting?' I will not help people to answer
those particular questions.

There was a story in a local newspaper about
gypsy families. The local council chairman said that
he was 'very unhappy at the way gypsies lived. They
ought to be like ordinary people and settle down
and send their children to normal schools.' The gypsy
leader replied robustly, 'We don't want to become like
the gorgios [non gypsies]. Their women do not
respect their menfolk any more. We do not like their
crime and sexual permissiveness. They have loose
ways.'

Each statement arrived like a lance in a jousting
tournament. It erected a barrier and judgment about
the other which prevented any effective

communication by applying personally held standards
and lifestyles as if they were Mosaic Law. Each
statement was an answer rather than a question — it
helped to close doors rather than to open them.

Taoism is different. Maslow defined 'taoistic' as
meaning

> self-regulation, self-government and the self-choice
> of the organism. . . . Taoistic means asking rather
> than telling. It means non-intruding, non-
> controlling. It stresses non-interfering observation
> rather than controlling manipulation. It is receptive
> and passive rather than active and forceful.[15]

It assumes that the other side has a reasonable
point of view — a slice of the truth. It is opposed to
people management and has no hard and delineated
aims in its relations to people. It is optimistic about
the nature of human beings. It holds that the organism
naturally searches for both physical and mental
health.

Taoistic means listening carefully, trying to
understand. This listening has an open heart; it is not
poisoned by the strong potions of jealousy, greed,
envy and aggression. Maslow described taoistic
methods of child-rearing. The best pathway for
children and parents was to 'develop techniques for
getting them to tell us what is best for them'.[16] But
that great wisdom involves a considerable subjugation
of our will; our dogmatism that *we really know* what
is best for other people, particularly our own
children.

There is much taoism in Virginia Axline's excellent
book.[17] It is a brief and enlightening account of
psychotherapy with a small child originally classified

as defective on referral.

> I attempted to keep my comments in line with his
> activity, trying not to say anything that would
> indicate any desire on my part that he do any
> particular thing, but rather to communicate,
> understandingly and simply, recognition in line
> with his frame of reference. I wanted him to lead
> the way. I would follow.

The therapist was firmly and clearly respecting the
child's knowledge of himself, particularly his capacity
for choosing healthy directions. She was continuously
giving permission to pursue certain pathways,
enlarging areas of choice gently and gradually without
imposing her own personal and very powerful
energies and will.

Community work also has its taoistic elements.
Professor Batten developed what he described as 'the
non-directive approach'.[18] In the directive approach,
the worker persuaded communities to 'accept the
results of his thinking for them, and the more he provides for them, the less they need to think, decide, and
provide for themselves. Thus he deprives them of
many potentially valuable learning experiences and
tends to make them more dependent on himself.'

This is yet another way in which the helpful worker
can undermine people's confidence in their
autonomy. A community worker can emerge as 'the
expert' who knows a great many of the answers and
so further undermines the community in very subtle
ways. The non-directive worker tries to increase
people's skills and knowledge of communication
processes. His emphasis is on developing ways of
expressing and articulating felt needs, on formulating

agreed objectives, priorities and methods. This type
of method encourages from the outset the growth of
indigenous leadership. He does not necessarily feel
he knows the answer to the problems. His function
is to listen and to guide in the direction of articulating
and expressing general wishes rather than his own.

Saul Alinsky, another great community worker,
was as different as possible in style and personality
from Batten. He could be both brooding and
aggressive. The Rama Indians asked for his help in
raising their depressed status and dealing with the
overall repression of the Canadian Indian Acts. In the
film I saw, they grumbled at length to Alinsky about
a wide variety of grievances, mostly blaming the
White Man. He listened impatiently and kept asking
what prices were they prepared to pay for social
change.

'What are you Indians going to do about this
situation? What costs are you prepared to meet?'
They had seen him as an outsider who would achieve
something for them; who knew the answers. He
pushed the problem back. He did not have to live
with legal repression and stigmatization. He accused
the Indians of wanting the economic and political
choices of the paleface but also desiring to hang on to
the ecological purity of their red ancestors.[19]

It is very hard to flow in the way Batten and
Alinsky did. It becomes harder still to give up those
ambitions for the control and changing of others; the
simple desire to appear important, to have influence,
to be popular and lovable. The sun simply shines
and the rain rains. It does not shine or rain in order
to annoy me when I wish to go for a walk or to
impress me when I sunbathe.

I feel this powerful urge to tell people what to do.

There is a great drive deep inside to manage people's lives, that only I know what really ought to happen. Hard-shelled ego. Often I would rather pretend that controlling desire is not there at all. It mainly feeds and enlarges my own pot-bellied ego.

Some years ago in Edinburgh, I had a fast and furious argument with a social work colleague. It became ego-fencing. She argued 'How can your precious and irrelevant religious ideas be relevant to a large industrial city like this with all its isolation? Yours are rural ideas where there is plenty of time and place.' I got angrier whilst she told me a story about a childless couple where the husband was a terrible alcoholic.

'Every night he comes home and beats her up black and blue. He's so violent and abusive. He'll really damage her one day.' I asked her which of the two had asked her to visit. 'Neither. This is the awful fact. Things are so bad that neither husband nor wife, whom I mostly see, view this drinking or beating up as much of a social problem.' She went on to explain that both people wanted her to stop visiting but that she persevered. Angrily I argued that she was then visiting largely *for her own good*; out of her own feelings of anxiety and guilt. This colleague became very cross. But both she and I might feel that people ought not to live in that way, to have greater respect for one another. Did we then have the right to intervene formally in the lives of those who break rules which we have made?

For whose benefit is the intervention/interference? Helpers can be guilty of attempting to alleviate their own problems or of the very worst kind of mental hygiene — brushing up the world to 'make it nice and tidy'. But that is still our conception of the world not that of our clients. My old social work tutor once said to me: 'David, always make sure you avoid treating yourself at the expense of the clients.'

The treatment is frequently worse than the disease. Chuang Tzu was refreshingly clear about his own position in the brief essay 'Leaving Things Alone'.[20]

> I know about leaving the world alone, not interfering. I do not know about running things. Leaving things alone: so that men will not blow their nature out of shape! Not interfering, so that men will not be changed into something they are not! When men do not get twisted and maimed beyond all recognition, when they are allowed to live — the purpose of government is achieved.

Chuang Tzu found his true nature.

Bill Jordan, over two thousand years later, describes some of the dangers of social work intervention. He was talking about the problems of child abuse.

> Very often referral agents increase the temptation by being deliberately vague, simply offloading their anxieties. . . . And if the social worker really does begin to feel anxiety that the children are at risk, this process can insidiously be carried a stage further, still without clarification of what is going on. The family can become a case, to be visited in a vague supervisory way, to check up, for the social worker to cover herself. The danger here is that rather than helping, the social worker can instead become part of the client's nightmare. The situation is never defined; the reason for supervision is never spelt out; the problem is never

brought out into the open. I feel sure myself that
these are the bases for the following research
findings: firstly, that when a comparison is made
between people receiving long-term casework
supervision and people with similar problems
receiving none, most of the people receiving
supervision get worse; and secondly, that as applied
to baby battering, anxious visiting by social
workers of families actually increases battering. In
the tragic cases we've all heard too much about,
the clients were not new referrals who hadn't been
investigated quickly enough, but cases known to
the department for a considerable period.[21]

Not to intervene at all can be the best form of
action.[22] Research into the results of intervening,
through group-work, psychotherapy and even
community development programmes, makes very
depressing reading. We need to review not only the
end result but also the motivating energy. Why did
we seek to intervene at all? Was it a simple expression
of our feelings that we were right and the desire to
'have our own way'?

We can work in a crude allegorical manner — seeing
different interest groups as either 'goodies' or
'baddies'. Communication can become just like that
between the gypsy leader and the council chairman.
We can erect solid barriers against those who are
perceived as harmful, destructive, left or right wing
or uncaring.

The whole process of change aimed at striving
towards desired goals, which are perceived as being
frustrated by hostile outsiders with vested interests,
has deep within itself the seeds of its own destruction
and disintegration. Those outsiders, labelled

frustrating and hostile, are a reflection of my craving
to have things my way. They want things their way.
How unreasonable can you get?

I can actually gain greater and wider influence by
lobbying harder and writing more; through promotion
and increased responsibility. Often I gain such
influence at the expense of others like my colleagues
in the same organization. The costs of gaining
influence can be an ever increasing loss of contact
with everyday events and a belief that I am more
important than others. Frequently, this process of
social and political climbing can result in a real social
aridity, an erosion of the capacity to love, to see
people, not as useful objects or tools to accomplish,
but simply as having value within themselves.

I cannot see the changes which occur in me.
Positions of power help me to shape and mould
others. So many senior professionals have become
very much like the senior colleagues they derided and
attacked only a decade before. We give up our
individual pursuit of the truth in return for the
comfort obtained from servicing the administrative
machines.

Struggling to change things can also have some of
the quality of George Orwell's *Animal Farm*. Turning
the wheel of fortune can simply result in lining our
pockets and dumping a different group of people in
the farmyard muck, thereby achieving no significant
change. We must not confuse our personal success
with general progress in the community.

Real change must begin inside myself. Reich
describes it beautifully:

> To start from self does not mean to be selfish. It
> means to start from premises based on human life

and the rest of nature, rather than premises that
are the artificial products of the Corporate State,
such as power or status. It is not an 'ego trip' but
a radical subjectivity designed to find genuine
values in a world whose official values are false and
distorted. It is not egocentricity, but honesty,
wholeness, genuineness in all things. It starts from
self because human life is found as individual units,
not as corporations and institutions; its intent is to
start from life.[23]

I believe in the essential subversive and
revolutionary nature of human love. We can begin
our revolution by exploiting each other less today;
by avoiding manipulative devices however difficult
that may be in a society which treats people as
industrial units rather than as individual human
beings.

Revolutions begin by some people living them;
experiencing different and more integrative feelings
about their relations to the outside world. They
happen by some people giving up their cherished
personal comfort and taking risks. If I desire real
change, I must first be prepared for change in myself.

Programmes of a political nature are important and
products of social quality that can be effective
only if the underlying structure of social values is
right. The social values are right only if the
individual values are right. The place to improve
the world is first in one's own heart and head and
hands, and then work outside from there.[24]

More important than seeking out refined and
sophisticated techniques and strategies for social

change, is an examination of why we desire it at all. Will such a change make us more comfortable, powerful or wealthy? Is it simply important to have our own way? As much dogmatic passion flows through my veins as most people's. There are enormous inequalities in our society and these are linked with mountains of individual suffering. Single parents bring up their children in severe poverty. Homeless families live communally in depressingly low-standard accommodation with dirty toilets and cramped washing facilities. Hundreds of homeless single men and women sleep out under the bridges of central London.

We have to live honestly and daily with the sheer crushing immensity of human suffering both national and international. We realize that our whole way of life, like that of every other 'major civilization' is based on sophisticated and organized theft of the world's resources from 'underdeveloped countries'. Pain and suffering begin inside ourselves. We too are lost, alienated and exploited.

What is called affluence — the consequence of the type of rapid economic development which occurred from about the middle of the nineteenth century — is in a real sense an abundance not just of serious problems which machines cannot solve, but of hopeless poverty: the physical insecurity, personal unhappiness, the intensified morality, the sense of being dwarfed by vast and uncontrollable physical, mechanical and corporate structures, the hatred and contempt of other peoples, the lack of opportunity for contemplation, the loss of community life.[25]

This is the extent of our brutalization and yet we see only the poverty of others. Sheldon Kopp argues that 'overcoming by yielding is the only escape'.[26] There is simply nowhere to escape from. To bring down the barriers, to insist less on the divisions between oneself and others, and making less dogmatic judgments must be illuminating for all. To allow the river to flow in its own direction and finding one's own nature feels right. To look deeply at my craving to change things is one beginning.

7 Zen fruit

What is Zen in the art of helping? It is easier to say
what it is not than more positively to describe the
essence. It is to avoid the boosting of the ego through
'good works'. It is to aid oneself and others in the
pursuit of the good life; to discover and uncover new
vigour and freshness in the art of living; to uncover
the primal ability of love.

Living in the here and now is a major ingredient.
This means concentrating more fully on tasks as they
are being done rather than longing for them to be
over. Normally we live our lives sandwiched in time
between important events. The decision as to what
is important and exciting is ours. Most of our living
goes by almost without noticing. We are scarcely
aware of washing-up or cleaning the car except in
occasional flashes.

These 'small' activities can reward attention. As
one Zen text has it:

> To wish for a fuller, happier life than your present
> one is natural and commendable. What is not
> commendable is to despise your present state
> while yearning for a more exalted one. In giving
> yourself over wholly to whatever you are doing at
> the moment you can achieve a deeper and richer
> state of mind.[1]

All of us have experience of the Cinderella process — wishing that we could go to the dance rather than do the washing-up. As a child, I struggled against my father's rapid flowing, seemingly drowning torrent of words. As I wished to get on with more 'important' activities, he would talk and talk until I screamed inside. In time, I learned to withdraw mentally — to complete arithmetical puzzles, recite poetry, travel to distant places — all to occupy the time silently whilst he talked on.

Through such mental gymnastics, I avoided the building up of frustration. I prevented myself from experiencing boredom. I took myself away from the here-and-now situation and evaded dealing with him directly. This split prevented me from seeing my father and helped in the use of him as a bogyman for many years. Concentration on the waves of words could have meant a challenging of my processes for deciding what was important as well as experiencing more fully enormous frustrations.

The Zen Master tries to provide an atmosphere of safety in which the student can find his true nature largely through concentration in the nowness. Too much safety however can induce slothful comfort and spiritual sleep. The Master tries to balance safety and challenge.

Learning Zen is largely unlearning. There is great pain in discovering that those ideological and intellectual monuments, giving a web of meaning to life, carefully constructed over a lifetime are quite insubstantial; that they fail to provide direct answers to the important questions in life. 'Who am I?' 'What is the nature of life?'

For me, becoming unattached from those personal monuments is much more difficult than detachment

from more 'worldly' goods. Irmgard Schloegl writes
'In the training, one must strive to give up everything
— and the stress here is on the "inner acquisitions",
such as notions and views and convictions rather than
on goods and chattels.'[2] I find that frightening.

Helping ourselves and others is complicated by the
situation and voracious appetite of the ego. It will
feed off anything and everything. It (or rather 'I')
comes between the experiencing of life and the real
desire to be liberated and enlightened. Even the most
seemingly pure of thoughts and deeds can be subtly
transmuted into self-righteousness. Doing good to
others can make me feel even more conscious of the
separation between myself and others. 'I' can become
proud of my own acquisition of personal virtue and
feel superior to others.

Fritz Perls, the founder of Gestalt therapy, was well
aware of this process. He related Zen principles to
psychotherapy. He offered his patients little help of
the comforting kind. They experienced an almost
X-ray concentration on the nowness of their words
and movements.[3] Frequently he was, by conventional
judgments, unhelpful. He attempted to increase the
frustration of his patients. He tried to extend their
personal awareness of the agony of Samsara — the
circle of self-frustrating effort — so that their ego
chains might suddenly burst in the released energy.
He made them seek their own internalized guru rather
than lean on him.

Perls realized the paradox of the will in Zen. It is
essential to want very badly to be enlightened but
that wanting and craving is a primary source of
energy for the ego. The ego seeks to make others do
the real work through continual questioning as well
as using any answers to further stockade itself against

possible attack.

> The psychiatrist asked the Zen Master: 'How do you deal with neurotics?' He replied simply, 'I trap them.'
> 'But how?', pressed the psychiatrist.
> He replied, 'I get them to where they cannot ask any more questions.'[4]

Perls realized that questions are our great intellectual escape from the pathway of personal discovery. We seek to seduce others into doing our work and suffering. Most of our questions are concealed statements. We procrastinate by pretending we do not know. That old rascal Bodhidarma is supposed to have said 'All know the Way, few walk it.' He might have added that those who do not walk it cry out regularly 'Show me . . . give me a map . . . which way is it?'

One aid to genuine helping is in refusing to answer many questions. This compels the students to use their own rich experience of life to explore the question. The answer of another is at best a 'knowing about' whilst your own reply is 'direct knowing'.

A contemporary Buddhist sage wrote:

> Now you may be thinking that people ask questions in order to dispel their doubts and clear up mental confusions and arrive at the truth, and admittedly this does sometimes happen. But most of the time people ask questions in order *not* to receive an answer. A real live answer is the last thing they want. Even if they got it they would not know what to do with it. Probably they would feel like a small boy playing at hunting lions and tigers in

the garden who was suddenly confronted by a real
live lion or tiger escaped from the zoo. So they go
on asking questions.[5]

I suggested earlier that much of our helping came
from the source of pity rather than compassion. Pity
is a giving which sees the giver as in some way
superior to the recipient. Compassion reduces the
barriers and contains genuine respect, as equals, from
one to the other.

I threw George, a Soho wino, out of the hostel
where I worked some years ago. I felt sorry for him
but he was very drunk as usual and being
troublesome to one of the women residents. There
was a short scuffle and then I bolted the large, main
door behind him.

Several hours later I passed him sitting on the steps
of a local church. He was with several Skid Row
friends and they were passing round a bottle of cheap
sherry. I thought there was going to be some trouble
but we chatted amiably about the events earlier in the
evening. I saw him for the first time, through the
clouds of pity, as an intelligent, sensitive man.

Compassion lies at the heart of genuine helping.
Often our helping is born out of personal desperation;
we go around pretending that we are not sick, nursing
those who are also unwell. Helping can be a
fundamental symptom of sickness, especially where it
is used to conceal our own inadequacies.

HELPING YOU?

The only way
I can let you know
that I need your help

is to insist
on helping you.

There is a kind of giving which springs from deep in
our hearts. Chögyam Trungpa sees most of life as
collecting objects and ideas rather than giving.

If we reconsider our spiritual shopping, can we
remember an occasion when we gave something
completely and properly, opened ourselves and
gave everything?[6]

Such giving seeks no reward. It is without intent,
design or calculation. It flows from us almost
bewilderingly and so swallows us up within the
process that there is no external reflection until the
completion.
Traditionally we see ourselves as quite outside the
changing process. There is that which is changing and
ourselves. The reality is different. R.D. Laing writes:

Soon as we interplay with the situation, we have
already begun to intervene willy nilly. Moreover
our intervention is already beginning to change us,
as well as the situation. A reciprocal relationship
has begun.[7]

Where do I begin and end in relationship to both
change and the whole situation?
Broadly, theories of helping both people and
society have posed a choice between extremely wide
and extremely narrow perspectives. Advocates of
political change have talked about altering social
structures and the balance of political power because
of the fundamentally exploitative nature. They have

had very little to say about the immediate suffering of the many except to assign them rather blandly to the socio-political limbo between the present moment and the coming of the Revolution. They offer a political opiate.

Caseworkers and psychotherapists have reached out to the present suffering of individuals and often accurately have been accused of adjusting people to intolerable and unjust social conditions rather than effecting genuine social change. As C. Wright Mills wrote, social workers 'have an occupationally trained incapacity to rise above a series of "cases".'[8] They fail to see the extent of the role of structural forms in the difficulties of the individuals.

A recent social work textbook accordingly criticizes the influence of psychoanalysis:

Psychoanalysis provided a skill which was rewarding to the social worker, who felt helpless before problems which were the results of political decisions and material deprivation. It encouraged a feeling that something could be done, and gave to the newly emergent profession a distinct skill distinguishing them from the layman and the amateur. Social problems became individualized, and the profession became immersed in an ideology which devalued collective political action. The poor and the deviants had progressed from moral inferiority to pathology.[9]

Social change or adjustment? This is a false dilemma on two levels. Each helper must help where and in the way that he can. We can certainly have aspirations and dreams about our helping but they are mainly important in the way they influence our actions in the present time.

This dilemma stems from seeing individuals as somehow separated from society. Here are individuals and over there are political and administrative structures. However, social institutions are themselves formed and made up from the behaviour and beliefs of thousands and thousands of individuals, some dead and some alive. Social institutions are dependent, in large part, on those living individuals who form their memberships. Strategies for change must achieve a balance between the liberating of individuals and the translation of that liberation into fairer and less repressive institutions.

Genuine helping cannot simply be restricted within the bounds of intrapsychic probing. It must mean intervening or even interfering in the social and economic situations and environment towards making it possible to lead the good life. Although leading the good life may not necessarily, as the Gospel of St. Matthew reminds us, be related to the accumulation of material goods.

There is a politics of experience as well as one of social structures. There are feelings concerned with power traced in my mind and heart and, in a diffusive way, dependant on the limits of personal influence, I attempt to balance what I perceive happening 'out there' with what goes on inside my head. Like King Lear, I attempt to achieve some equilibrium between outside and inside by making changes inside myself as well as through attempting to manipulate the outside world.

Structurally, I feel depressed and despondent about the nature of my profession. It seems that the possibilities for effectively helping clients are so restricted. However, I am surrounded by colleagues who achieve really effective contact. I seem to be helping and am helped by many social work students.

It is difficult to see the world. Many parts of it have already been 'decided' by me. I have arrived at a series of standards and filters which are indicated by an almost continuous stream of judgments on the experiences I have of it. I am dimly aware of selecting and excluding much material.

This morning it is raining and dull and I had decided to go for a walk in the country near my home. So I decide to write and am continually interrupted by the children who wish me to play with them. Life is always letting me down. It fails to live up to my prescriptions of what it should be.

Many Buddhists see the whole basis of 'neurosis' in the attempt to form a barrier separating space into two divisions — 'I' and 'Other'. In achieving this separation 'I' makes judgments about the character and nature of the outside world — that it is threatening, attractive or uninteresting.

Ichazo describes the growth of this process:

A contradiction develops between the inner feelings of the child and the outer social reality to which he must conform. Ego consciousness is the limited awareness that develops as a result of the fall into society. Personality forms a defensive layer over the essence and so there is a split between the self and the world. The ego feels the world is alien and dangerous because it constantly fails to satisfy the deeper needs of the self.[10]

There are many different responses to this central dissatisfaction and threat. Some people fear being surprised, confused or overwhelmed by the outside.

They try to keep the outside world at a considerable distance by using abstract intellectualization and 'objectivity' or more simply through cold or hot anger. Others try to take over the outside world by incorporating it as a part of their own territory and thus become overbearing, mothering and imperious.

One approach is to seduce the outside and get encaptured in a sensuous experiencing of complexities and intricacies. Another group attempts to control the external by direct manipulation from a fear of being attacked or of being alone and outside. Yet another group becomes dulled and have their energies frozen and are smug and complacent.

Satori or awakening consists in melting away those barriers which separate us from the outside world. It lies in a direct perception of reality. Thomas Keefe writes that this means

> holding cognitive processes in temporary abeyance and allowing things and others to speak for themselves — gives rise to critical re-orientation of the helping person's approach to others. One's capacity for empathy is enhanced. The self is no longer separated from the world and others as experiencer. One does not watch one's self interact and react with the mind's eye. Experience is unified. The skier, for example, is skiing but not watching himself skiing; his ego is not preoccupied with, but wholly consumed by, the action.[11]

Change is happening all around us, in us and through us. Our purposeful intent to change, however well intentioned, can hinder genuine development through enhancing the size of the ego rather than assisting in its disintegration. Any change

requires some belief that it is possible; some facility
to see that it is happening. Often that belief and
facility are missing. People's morale has become so
low; they feel so bad that they cannot any longer
believe in genuine change except for the worse. Life
can become a chain of self-fulfilling prophecies.

There is a Zen story about a woman who could not
make up her mind out of which door she would leave
a particular room. Both doors led to the outside
world. After some hours of indecision she piled up
some mats against one of the exits and fell fast
asleep. Early in the morning she got up and surveyed
the whole problem again. One door was free but the
other was blocked by a heap of mats. She sighed at
length 'Now I have no choice.'

Part of the role of the helper is to bring people to
an awareness that there are choices to be made at
all. That is the importance of the work of Paulo
Freiro, Ivan Illich and Che Guevara. This means
helping people to realize the extent of their
oppression and exploitation. Both oppressor and
oppressed are caught in the same trap. Radicals
rightly shout about the ways in which the exploited
are demeaned by their experience. But in a more
subtle and certainly more materially comfortable way
so are the oppressors. In the process of exploitation
both oppressors and oppressed have an essential part of
their dignity eroded. Their actions are reflections of
fear and insecurity.

Manipulation hinders the authentic growth of
both. My experience as a helper, but more poignantly
as one who has been helped, gives me a great
confidence in the community's own ability for
caring. Love is all around. Helpers are in a real sense,
people who sell water by the river. Compassion flows

all around them although we find it difficult to channel and irrigate it.

We begin to revolutionize society by removing obstacles to greater caring from within ourselves. We are all concerned to increase the overall quantity of caring within the community. Much harm and exploitation comes from unintended sources. We may disagree vehemently on the nature of human caring and certainly about the means of increasing it.

Caring leads us outwards to consider whether or not we have appropriated too much of the world's goods and resources. How can we more fairly spread the opportunities for good housing, fuller employment and better education? Our political structures seem frequently to reflect greed and ambition rather than caring.

Love begins in individual hearts. We have not yet uncovered ways to amplify it into benevolent administrative structures. Size seems one important aspect. The larger the organization, the more lost and alienated I feel. I can rarely feel that I matter in dealings with a large organization with so many rules, regulations and written codes of communication.

A friend told me that she went to order a gas cooker from the showrooms. To her amazement, the salesman said that the delivery of any model in the catalogue or on display would take six months or more. She pleaded with him, more and more seductively — surely it must be possible to get the cooker in less time than that? Hers was a special case. Finally he took her round the other side of his counter and there she saw a printed notice underneath his desk which said simply: 'Never promise any customer delivery of a cooker in under six months.'

It seems that discussions and contact are between roles rather than persons. We touch each other only in carefully defined and prescribed rituals. We pass carefully prepared scripts across the desks and in the interviewing rooms. In such systems people get lost. The drive for objectivity, rationality and efficiency sucks away my humanness. I am left more lonely than before.

My nowness is that sense of isolation. Institutions seem so un-now. They are continually making decisions and drawing up plans for things which may happen at some far distant time. 'What will we do if. . . .?' As if they did not trust themselves corporately to react effectively when that moment arrives. I feel mischievously that I would like to release a horde of rampant armadillos and see whether government had contingency plans for that.

Government is concerned about economic efficiency as well as contact with consumers. It tries to evolve as well as to evaluate policies, which in the helping field anyway, are to do with allocating scarce resources. These policies are said to be about distributing the social goods more equitably especially to those with large families, single parents and handicapped and elderly. Looking at the low level of welfare benefits, the humiliation of the recipients and the low proportion of those who receive compared with those who are entitled, such policies must be judged a failure.

I agree with Schumacher's thesis in *Small is Beautiful.* He argues that there is a need for very much smaller institutions and structures. In a chapter entitled 'Buddhist Economics' he writes

The Buddhist point of view takes the function of

work to be three fold; to give a man a chance to utilise and develop his faculties; to enable him to overcome his egocentredness by joining with other people in a common task; and to bring forth the goods and services for a becoming existence. . . . consumption is merely a means to human well-being, the aim should be to obtain the maximum of well-being with the minimum of consumption.[12, 13]

It is difficult to see how a growth in the geographical and administrative size of commercial and governmental structures can help a corresponding growth in respect for and appreciation of individual human differences and identities. As I suggested earlier, the growth of professions may do much to undermine people's confidence in their own autonomy if they result in the establishment of an 'expertise in living'. The combination of large professions and administrative structures can increase the individual's experience of his powerlessness.

The traveller walks the Middle Way. He sees the need for the fairer allocation of resources and watches whether such institutions achieve that process. He observes the need for the development of professions to foster skills and ethical codes of practice and measures the cost of iatrogenesis.

Genuine helping aims to liberate both helper and helped. But helping can frequently result in the greater personal and structural enslavement of both. Our struggling can entangle us more deeply in the net of ego and suffering. We may seek to control others in the guise of helping them.

A councillor from Fife social work committee argued that authorities might more readily give

Zen fruit

houses to families if they were assured that there
would be a

> high measure of supervision by the social work
> department. In the case of my old authority . . .
> we found that adequate supervision was not
> always offered by the social work department.
> For example, one family rehoused by us cost us
> something in the order of £300 for repairs to the
> house. We must be able to give an assurance that
> there will be adequate supervision, and the houses
> will be well maintained.[14]

This is really to spell out the policing and controlling
functions of certain forms of helping.

Such examples of controlling 'helping' arouse the
anger of 'Anarchy'.

> Social workers are agents of the State; they don't
> wear uniforms — they are plain clothes cops and
> robbers. They supervise our homes and our manner
> of living. They rob us of our children, fucking us
> all up in the process. Controlling in the guise of
> protecting. . . . She [the social worker] doesn't
> offer to babysit or anything useful, it's just talk
> and useless sympathy.[15]

I take this comment, cartoon though it is, very
seriously. I sense attempts at a much greater degree of
control not only over clients but also over
professionals. It seems right that professionals should
become more accountable but the question is —
accountable to whom?

The professional helper is pulled in the different
directions of being increasingly responsive to

112

administrative structures and also his clients. He is
supposed to be a human channel for social
compassion whilst his agency uses him as a gatekeeper
to prevent what it sees as the possible looting of the
storehouse of resources by the consumers.

Words like liaison and co-ordinate emerge as
synonyms for control, particularly at times of
economic crisis and large-scale unemployment. This
control may have nothing to do with the development
of either economic or social efficiency. It may actually
be directed at escaping accountability for certain
sorts of human situations. The process of control
can be enormously wasteful of both human
compassion and enthusiasm by undermining people's
confidence unnecessarily, by crushing innovation and
creativity and by diverting more and more resources
away from the frontline.

Some tensions appear irreconcilable. I listened to a
student who organized the delivery of Christmas
parcels to pensioners. One elderly person complained
to me that she heard a loud knock at her door and by
the time she opened it there was nothing except a
large parcel of Christmas goods. My student explained
to me patiently that they did not wait to make
contact with the pensioner because it was 'more
efficient' to knock and continue their delivery.
Speedier it may have been but it effectively ruled out
the possibility for human contact which might have
been even more important than the parcel.

The most distressing part of the overall trend to
control and organize lies in the attempt to take over
both voluntary societies and community help. I went
to a large meeting of voluntary societies in
Lancashire organized by the local authority social

services department called 'Working Together'. After several hours of speeches, I was convinced that the more honest title should have been 'Working for Us'.

The large council chamber was dominated by local authority representatives. There was much talk about the contributions people (voluntary societies) could make to the hard-pressed social workers. Blue, pink and white forms were handed out to encourage volunteers to donate their services.

Apart from giving me a further opportunity to explore my own anger and arrogance, the conference fell into the trap of seeing informal community help as in some way supplementary to the local authority and professional effort. The representatives from the local authorities wanted to help by co-ordinating the voluntary effort to 'rationalise and prevent overlapping'.

These attempts mean well but they can kill off the humanness, the untidy organic affection of one to another. Inorganic interference can murder altruistic plants. Helping is less a task-oriented activity than an indication of a way of living and being. It is a process frequently springing from our everyday life and a retreat from controlling and shaping. Helping others is a good way of helping ourselves. There is a growth of continuity between self and others. Ego barriers melt and compassion can grow.

If we can see that the aim is also the process, we can stop to give the Christmas parcel to the pensioner. In our stopping we can learn simply to be rather than continuously striving after ego ideals which offer scant satisfaction or enlightenment. In the giving of the parcel we can ourselves receive.

This is not argument against the making of rules which may well be necessary. Informality and smallness of size are, in themselves, no guarantee at all of a genuine respect for persons. It is better if those rules are seen to emerge organically out of the daily lives of those to whom they are to apply. It is better if people can take on their own form of discipline whatever shape that takes. It is also good if the rules are guidelines rather than regulations; if they suggest areas of growth, flexibility and discretion rather than tightly define people's occupational function and social status.

There must always be conflicts between people's perceptions of their wants and needs and their case as viewed by the agents of the community. Social workers describe a family as inadequate which manages to survive on half the amount of money with twice as many children as professionals have. At least those agents can deal with their own needs to preserve an unequal society face to face with those who suffer the consequences of it as human beings rather than as bureaucrats.

The hard thing for me to do is to accept the bureaucrat in my own heart. He is there. Part of me wishes to control situations and to seek substantial influence over people's lives. Part of me screams out that I know best. Anger at large administrative institutions is one way of rejecting that controlling part.

The real greatness of Alexander Solzhenitsyn's book *The Gulag Archipelago* is not in the description of the horrifying inhumanity of man to man. The height of the book lies in his own recognition of that same kind of inhumanity in his past dealings with people. That awareness takes tremendous courage.[16]

The most genuine achievement is to accept our part of the responsibility. The most common way of

avoiding this is through the technique of blaming. 'It
wasn't me, it was those others. . . .' Michael Frayn
deals firmly with that issue.

> Our desire to blame and to be blamed is often an
> attempt to impose meaning upon events which
> offer none, or only an obscure and confusing one.
> For some impossibly complex conjunction of
> reasons, a lorry plunges into a crowd; an
> economic policy fails; a battle is lost. Our instinct
> is at once to find someone whose behaviour can
> now be reinterpreted as negligent or criminal, so
> that the event can be read into the world's great
> underlying pattern of cause and effect.[17]

Blaming people will not help us to reach out to
others. How can we make contact with and be
contacted in a way which will meet a little of our
needs? How can we combine the pursuit of influence
and love? How can we stop pursuing? Those
processes can be assisted more from our basic
intuition than from cognitive reflection. It is warmth
rather than wise words that crosses the many barriers.
Sheldon Kopp writes

> Research in self disclosure supports my own
> evidence that the personal openness of the guru
> facilitates the increased openness of the pilgrim.
> But I operate not to help the patient, but to help
> myself. It is from the centre of my own being that
> I am moved to share my tale. . . . I try to be guided
> by Carl Whitaker's advice to feed the patient not
> when he is crying that he is hungry, but only when
> I feel the milk overflowing from my own nipples.[18]

But Kopp writes as if the two responses of helping and being helped were quite separate. That does not correspond with my experience. Helping and being helped have tended to merge, become joyfully confused, interactive and entwined to the mutual benefit of both persons. If I can see that someone's distress is genuine (and I can be very insensitive and just plain wrong) I feel, most often, a wanting to care and open my heart.

Notes

Chapter 1: Introduction

1 M.H. Trevor (trans.), *The Ox and His Herdsman — a Chinese Zen Text*, Hokuseido Press, 1969, p. 95.
2 Matthew 8: 20.
3 David Brandon, *Homeless*, Sheldon Press, 1974.
4 Lucein Stryk *et al.* (eds), *Zen Poems of China and Japan — the Cranes Bill*, Anchor Books, 1973, p. 90.
5 Leo Tolstoy, *What then must we do?* (trans. Maude and Aylmer), Oxford University Press, 1975.

Chapter 2: What is Zen?

1 R.H. Blyth, *Zen and Zen Classics*, vol. 4, *Mumonkan*, Hokuseido Press, 1966, p.42.
2 Alan Watts, *The Way of Zen*, Penguin Books, 1972, pp. 104—5.
3 Heinrich Dumoulin, *A History of Zen Buddhism*, Random House, 1963, p. 67.
4 Daisetz Suzuki, *Zen and Japanese Culture*, Princeton University Press, 1970.
5 R.H. Blyth, *Zen in English Literature and Oriental Classics*, Dutton, 1960.
6 Eugen Herrigel, *Zen in the Art of Archery*, Routledge & Kegan Paul, 1953.
7 Daisetz Suzuki, Foreword, *Introduction to Zen Buddhism*, Rider, 1949.
8 R.H. Blyth, *Zen and Zen Classics*, vol. 4, Mumonkan, p. 147.
9 Irmgard Schloegl (trans.), *The Record of Rinzai*, Buddhist Society, 1975, p. 9.

10 A.F. Price and Mou-Lam Wong (trans.) *The Sutra of of Hui Neng*, Shambala, 1969, p. 25.
11 Thomas Merton, *The Zen Revival*, Buddhist Society, 1967, p. 14.
12 Paul Reps (compiler), *Zen Flesh, Zen Bones*, Tuttle, 1971, p. 74.
13 R.H. Blyth, *Zen in English Literature and Oriental Classics*, Dutton, 1960, p. 216.
14 Paul Reps, *op. cit.*, p. 165.
15 Daisetz Suzuki, *The Zen Doctrine of No Mind*, Rider, 1949, p. 89.
16 R.H. Blyth, *Zen and Zen Classics*, vol. 4, Momonkan, p. 44.
17 Thomas Merton, *The Way of Chuang Tzu*, Allen & Unwin, 1970.
18 J. Krishnamurti, *You are the World*, Krishnamurti Foundation, 1972.
19 Idries Shah, *The Exploits of the Incomparable Mulla Nasrudin*, Jonathan Cape, 1966.
20 Thomas Merton, *Zen and the Birds of Appetite*, New Directions Publications, 1968.
21 Thomas Merton, *The Wisdom of the Desert*, Sheldon Press, 1974, p. 30.
22 *Ibid.*, p. 62.
23 Daisetz Suzuki, *Essays in Zen Buddhism,*(first series), Rider, 1949, pp. 268—9.

Chapter 3: Hindering

1 Bernard Shaw, *The Doctor's Dilemma*, 1906, Act I.
2 Philip Slater, *The Pursuit of Loneliness — American Culture at Breaking Point*, Penguin Books, 1975, pp. 154—5.
3 Williard C. Richan and Allan Mendelsohn, *Social Work — the Unloved Profession*, New Viewpoints, Franklin Watts, 1973, p. 16.
4 John Nurse, 'The Client, the Caseworker and the Absent Third Person', *British Journal of Social Work*, Spring 1973, pp. 39—53.
5 David Brandon, *Homeless*, Sheldon Press, 1974.
6 Ivan Illich, *Medical Nemesis*, Calder & Boyars, 1975, p. 25.

Notes

7 Herschel Prins, 'Motivation in Social Work', *Social Work Today*, vol. 5, 18:4:1974.

8 Ivan Illich, *ibid.*, pp. 26—7

9 David Brandon, 'Confidentiality in Social Work?' *Community Care*, 23:4:1975.

10 Geoffrey Pearson, 'Making Social Workers: Bad Promises and Good Omens', in Roy Bailey and Mike Brake (eds) *Radical Social Work*, Arnold, 1975, p. 30.

11 Anthony Bloom, 'Yoga and Christian Spiritual Techniques', in Pitrim A. Sorokin (ed.), *Forms and Techniques of Altruistic and Spiritual Growth*, Beacon Press, 1954, p. 97.

12 Michael Frayn, *Constructions*, Wildwood House, 1974, p. 32.

13 G.M. Aves, *The Voluntary Worker in the Social Services*, Allen & Unwin, 1969 (Aves Report), p. 171.

14 Bill Jordan, *The Social Worker in Family Situations*, Routledge & Kegan Paul, 1972, p. 136.

15 Williard C. Richan and Allan Mendelsohn, *op. cit.*, p. 9.

16 Noel Timms and J. Mayer, *The Client Speaks*, Routledge & Kegan Paul, 1970.

17 J.E. Neill *et al.*, 'Reactions to Integration', *Social Work Today*, 4(15), 458—65.

18 Michael Bayley, *Mentally Handicapped and the Community*, Routledge & Kegan Paul, 1973.

19 Alexander Solzhenitsyn, *Cancer Ward*, Bodley Head, 1968, pp. 85—7.

20 Tony Smythe and Denise Winn, from *Mind Out*, journal of Mind Campaign, no. 10 (April 1975).

21 Ivan Illich, *op. cit.*, p. 165.

22 J.E. Neill *et al.*, *op. cit.*

23 David Brandon, 'New Careers — social judo?, *Community Care*, 23:10:1974.

24 Irmgard Schloegl, *The Wisdom of the Zen Masters*, Sheldon Press, 1975, p. 12.

Chapter 4: Compassion

1 Paul Reps (compiler), *Zen Flesh, Zen Bones*, Penguin Books, 1971, pp. 49—50.

2 Bentz Plagemann, *My Place to Stand*, Farrar Strauss,
     1949, p. 9.
3 Chögyam Trungpa, *Cutting through Spiritual Materialism*,
     Stuart & Watkins, 1973, p. 99.
4 Christmas Humphreys, *A Western Approach to Zen*, Allen
     & Unwin, 1971, p. 146.
5 Philip Kapleau (ed.), *The Three Pillars of Zen*, Harper &
     Row, 1966, p. 44.
6 Erich Fromm, *The Art of Loving*, Harper & Row, 1956,
     p. 20.
7 Herschel Prins, 'Motivation in Social Work', *Social Work
     Today*, vol. 5, no. 2, 18:4:1974.
8 Philip Kapleau (ed.), *The Three Pillars of Zen*, p. 140.
9 Erich Fromm, *op. cit.*, p. 74.
10 D.C. Lau (trans.), *Lao Tzu — Tao Te Ching*, Penguin
     Books, 1972, p. 64.
11 Erich Fromm, *op. cit.*, p. 22.
12 R.H. Blyth, *Zen in English Literature and Oriental Classics*,
     Dutton, 1960, p. 95.
13 *Ibid.*, p. 355.
14 Erich Fromm, *op. cit.*, p. 8.

Chapter 5: Nowness

1 Chögyam Trungpa, *Meditation in Action*, Stuart &
     Watkins, 1969, p. 52.
2 Thomas Keefe, 'A Zen Perspective on Social Casework',
     Social Casework (USA), March 1975.
3 Abraham Maslow, *The Farther Reaches of Human Nature*,
     Penguin Books, 1973, p. 103.
4 Carl Rogers, *Client Centred Therapy*, Houghton Mifflin,
     1965, pp. 48—9.
5 Herbert Guenther and Chögyam Trungpa, *The Dawn of
     Tantra*, Shambala, 1975, p. 83.
6 Abraham Maslow, *op. cit.*, p. 129.
7 Quoted in Michael Frayn, *Constructions*, Wildwood House,
     1974, para. 124.
8 Joen Fagen (ed.), *Gestalt Therapy Now*, Penguin Books,
     1973, see chapter 6, Arnold Beisser, 'The Paradoxical
     Theory of Change'.

Notes

9 R.H. Blyth, *Zen in English Literature and Oriental Classics*, Dutton, 1960, p. 101.
10 Paul Reps (compiler), *Zen Flesh, Zen Bones*, Penguin Books, 1971, p. 32.
11 Nobuyuki Yuasa (trans.), *The Narrow Road to the Deep North and other Travel Sketches*, Penguin Books, 1966, p. 33.

Chapter 6: Taoistic change

1 Chögyam Trungpa, *Meditation in Action*, Stuart & Watkins, 1969, p. 55.
2 Charles Reich, *The Greening of America*, Penguin Books, 1971, pp. 75—6.
3 Val Hennessy, letter to *New Society*, 'Free Children', 30:10:1975.
4 Charles Reich, *op. cit.*, p. 114.
5 Geoffrey Parrinder, *Man and his Gods*, Hamlyn, 1971, p. 283.
6 Chang Chung-yuan, *Creativity and Taoism*, Wildwood House, 1975, p. 36.
7 Rollo May, *Power and Innocence*, Norton (New York), 1972, pp. 21—3.
8 Howard Bahr, *Skid Row — an Introduction to Disaffiliation*, Oxford University Press, 1973.
9 Charles Reich, *op. cit.*, p. 242.
10 Paulo Freiro, *Cultural Action for Freedom*, Penguin Books, 1972, p. 51.
11 Thomas Merton, *The Way of Chuang Tzu*, Allen & Unwin, 1970, p. 28.
12 *Ibid.*, from the Introduction —p. 23.
13 R.H. Blyth, *Zen and Zen Classics*, vol 4, *Mumonkan*, Hokuseido Press, 1966, pp. 54—5.
14 *Ibid.*, pp. 304—5.
15 Abraham Maslow, *The Farther Reaches of Human Nature*, Penguin Books, 1973, p. 15.
16 *Ibid.*, p. 15.
17 Virginia Axline, *Dibs: In Search of Self*, Penguin Books, 1973.
18 T.R. Batten, *The Non-directive Approach in Group and Community Work*, Oxford University Press, 1971.

19 *Saul Alinsky: An Encounter with the Rama Indians*, (film).
20 Thomas Merton, *op. cit.*, p. 70.
21 Bill Jordan, 'Is the Client a Fellow Citizen?', Address to the British Association of Social Workers conference in Edinburgh, September 1975.
22 E.M. Schur, *Radical Non-Intervention*, Heinemann, 1973.
23 Charles Reich, *op. cit.*, p. 190.
24 Robert Pirsig, *Zen and the Art of Motorcycle Maintenance*, Bodley Head, 1974, p. 121.
25 C.R. Hensman, *Rich against Poor — the reality of aid*, Penguin Books, 1975, p. 51.
26 Sheldon Kopp, *If you meet the Buddha on the Road, Kill Him! — the pilgrimage of psychotherapy patients*, Sheldon Press, 1974, p. 46.

Chapter 7: Zen fruit

1 Philip Kapleau (ed.), *The Three Pillars of Zen*, Beacon Press, 1966, p. 142.
2 Irmgard Schloegl, *The Wisdom of the Zen Masters*, Sheldon Press, 1975, p. 25.
3 Fritz Perls, *Gestalt Therapy Verbatim*, Penguin Books, 1972.
4 Alan Watts, *Psychotherapy — East and West*, Penguin Books, 1973, p. 32.
5 Ven Maha Sthavira Sangharakshita, *The Essence of Zen*, Friends of the Western Buddhist Order, 1973, p. 26.
6 Chögyam Trungpa, *Cutting through Spiritual Materialism*, Stuart & Watkins, 1973, p. 81.
7 R.D. Laing, *Intervention in Social Situations*, Philadelphia Association, p. 16.
8 C.W. Mills, 'The Professional Ideology of Social Pathologists', *American Journal of Sociology*, vol. 49, no. 2, p. 171.
9 Roy Bailey and Mike Brake (eds.), *Radical Social Work*, Arnold, 1975, p. 6.
10 Sam Keen, 'A Conversation about Ego Destruction with Oscar Ichazo', *Psychology Today*, vol. 7, no. 2, July 1973.

Notes

11 Thomas Keefe, 'A Zen perspective on social casework',
    Social Casework, March 1975, pp. 140—4.
12 F.E. Schumacher, *Small is Beautiful*, Blond & Briggs,
    1973, p. 49.
13 *Ibid.*, p. 52.
14 *Guardian*, 8:11:1975.
15 Quoted in *Case con*, (magazine for revolutionary social
    workers) Spring 1975.
16 Alexander Solzhenitsyn, *The Gulag Archipelago*, (Part 1),
    Collins/Fontana, 1974 (chapter 14 — 'The Blue Caps').
17 Michael Frayn, *Constructions*, Wildwood House, 1974,
    para. 12.
18 Sheldon Kopp, *If you meet the Buddha on the Road, Kill
    Him! — the pilgrimage of psychotherapy patients*,
    Sheldon Press, 1974, p. 17.

ARKANA – NEW-AGE BOOKS FOR MIND, BODY AND SPIRIT

A selection of titles

With over 200 titles currently in print, Arkana is the leading name in quality new-age books for mind, body and spirit. Arkana encompasses the spirituality of both East and West, ancient and new, in fiction and non-fiction. A vast range of interests is covered, including Psychology and Transformation, Health, Science and Mysticism, Women's Spirituality and Astrology.

If you would like a catalogue of Arkana books, please write to:

Arkana Marketing Department
Penguin Books Ltd
27 Wright's Lane
London W8 5TZ

ARKANA – NEW-AGE BOOKS FOR MIND, BODY AND SPIRIT

A selection of titles

Neal's Yard Natural Remedies Susan Curtis, Romy Fraser and Irene Kohler

Natural remedies for common ailments from the pioneering Neal's Yard Apothecary Shop. An invaluable resource for everyone wishing to take responsibility for their own health, enabling you to make your own choice from homeopathy, aromatherapy and herbalism.

Zen in the Art of Archery Eugen Herrigel

Few in the West have strived as hard as Eugen Herrigel to learn Zen from a Master. His classic text gives an unsparing account of his initiation into the 'Great Doctrine' of archery. Baffled by its teachings he gradually began to glimpse the depth of wisdom behind the paradoxes.

The Absent Father: Crisis and Creativity Alix Pirani

Freud used Oedipus to explain human nature; but Alix Pirani believes that the myth of Danae and Perseus has most to teach an age which offers 'new responsibilities for women and challenging questions for men' – a myth which can help us face the darker side of our personalities and break the patterns inherited from our parents.

Woman Awake: A Celebration of Women's Wisdom Christina Feldman

In this inspiring book, Christina Feldman suggests that it *is* possible to break out of those negative patterns instilled into us by our social conditioning as women: conformity, passivity and surrender of self. Through a growing awareness of the dignity of all life and its connection with us, we can regain our sense of power and worth.

Water and Sexuality Michel Odent

Taking as his starting point his world-famous work on underwater childbirth at Pithiviers, Michel Odent considers the meaning and importance of water as a symbol: in the past – expressed through myths and legends – and today, from an advertisers' tool to a metaphor for aspects of the psyche.

ARKANA – NEW-AGE BOOKS FOR MIND, BODY AND SPIRIT

A selection of titles

The Revised Waite's Compendium of Natal Astrology
Alan Candlish

This completely revised edition retains the basic structure of Waite's classic work while making major improvements to accuracy and readability.

Aromatherapy for Everyone   Robert Tisserand

The therapeutic value of essential oils was recognized as far back as Ancient Egyptian times. Today there is an upsurge in the use of these fragrant and medicinal oils to soothe and heal both mind and body. Here is a comprehensive guide to every aspect of aromatherapy by the man whose name is synonymous with its practice and teaching.

Tao Te Ching ·The Richard Wilhelm Edition

Encompassing philosophical speculation and mystical reflection, the *Tao Te Ching* has been translated more often than any other book except the Bible, and more analysed than any other Chinese classic. Richard Wilhelm's acclaimed 1910 translation is here made available in English.

The Book of the Dead   E. A. Wallis Budge

Intended to give the deceased immortality, the Ancient Egyptian *Book of the Dead* was a vital piece of 'luggage' on the soul's journey to the other world, providing for every need: victory over enemies, the procurement of friendship and – ultimately – entry into the kingdom of Osiris.

Yoga: Immortality and Freedom   Mircea Eliade

Eliade's excellent volume explores the tradition of yoga with exceptional directness and detail.

'One of the most important and exhaustive single-volume studies of the major ascetic techniques of India and their history yet to appear in English' – *San Francisco Chronicle*

ARKANA – NEW-AGE BOOKS FOR MIND, BODY AND SPIRIT

A selection of titles

Weavers of Wisdom: Women Mystics of the Twentieth Century Anne Bancroft

Throughout history women have sought answers to eternal questions about existence and beyond – yet most gurus, philosophers and religious leaders have been men. Through exploring the teachings of fifteen women mystics – each with her own approach to what she calls 'the truth that goes beyond the ordinary' – Anne Bancroft gives a rare, cohesive and fascinating insight into the diversity of female approaches to mysticism.

Dynamics of the Unconscious: Seminars in Psychological Astrology Volume II Liz Greene and Howard Sasportas

The authors of *The Development of the Personality* team up again to show how the dynamics of depth psychology interact with your birth chart. They shed new light on the psychology and astrology of aggression and depression – the darker elements of the adult personality that we must confront if we are to grow to find the wisdom within.

The Myth of Eternal Return: Cosmos and History Mircea Eliade

'A luminous, profound, and extremely stimulating work . . . Eliade's thesis is that ancient man envisaged events not as constituting a linear, progressive history, but simply as so many creative repetitions of primordial archetypes . . . This is an essay which everyone interested in the history of religion and in the mentality of ancient man will have to read. It is difficult to speak too highly of it' – Theodore H. Gaster in *Review of Religion*

The Second Krishnamurti Reader Edited by Mary Lutyens

In this reader bringing together two of Krishnamurti's most popular works, *The Only Revolution* and *The Urgency of Change*, the spiritual teacher who rebelled against religion points to a new order arising when we have ceased to be envious and vicious. Krishnamurti says, simply: 'When you are not, love is.' 'Seeing,' he declares, 'is the greatest of all skills.' In these pages, gently, he helps us to open our hearts and eyes.

ARKANA – NEW-AGE BOOKS FOR MIND, BODY AND SPIRIT

A selection of titles

A Course in Miracles: The Course, Workbook for Students and Manual for Teachers

Hailed as 'one of the most remarkable systems of spiritual truth available today', *A Course in Miracles* is a self-study course designed to shift our perceptions, heal our minds and change our behaviour, teaching us to experience miracles – 'natural expressions of love' – rather than problems generated by fear in our lives.

Sorcerers Jacob Needleman

'An extraordinarily absorbing tale' – John Cleese.

'A fascinating story that merges the pains of growing up with the intrigue of magic . . . constantly engrossing' – *San Francisco Chronicle*

Arthur and the Sovereignty of Britain: Goddess and Tradition in the Mabinogion Caitlín Matthews

Rich in legend and the primitive magic of the Celtic Otherworld, the stories of the *Mabinogion* heralded the first flowering of European literature and became the source of Arthurian legend. Caitlín Matthews illuminates these stories, shedding light on Sovereignty, the Goddess of the Land and the spiritual principle of the Feminine.

Shamanism: Archaic Techniques of Ecstasy Mircea Eliade

Throughout Siberia and Central Asia, religious life traditionally centres around the figure of the shaman: magician and medicine man, healer and miracle-doer, priest and poet.

'Has become the standard work on the subject and justifies its claim to be the first book to study the phenomenon over a wide field and in a properly religious context' – *The Times Literary Supplement*

ARKANA – NEW-AGE BOOKS FOR MIND, BODY AND SPIRIT

A selection of titles

Head Off Stress: Beyond the Bottom Line D. E. Harding

Learning to head off stress takes no time at all and is impossible to forget – all it requires is that we dare take a fresh look at ourselves. This infallible and revolutionary guide from the author of *On Having No Head* – whose work C. S. Lewis described as 'highest genius' – shows how.

Shadows in the Cave Graham Dunstan Martin

We can all recognize our friends in a crowd, so why can't we describe in words what makes a particular face unique? The answer, says Graham Dunstan Martin, is that our minds are not just computers: drawing constantly on a fund of tacit knowledge, we always *know* more than we can ever *say*. Consciousness, in fact, is at the very heart of the universe, and – like the earth itself – we are all aspects of a single universal mind.

The Magus of Strovolos: The Extraordinary World of a Spiritual Healer Kyriacos C. Markides

This vivid account introduces us to the rich and intricate world of Daskalos, the Magus of Strovolos – a true healer who draws upon a seemingly limitless mixture of esoteric teachings, psychology, reincarnation, demonology, cosmology and mysticism, from both East and West.

'This is a really marvellous book . . . one of the most extraordinary accounts of a "magical" personality since Ouspensky's account of Gurdjieff' – Colin Wilson

Meetings With Remarkable Men G. I. Gurdjieff

All that we know of the early life of Gurdjieff – one of the great spiritual masters of this century – is contained within these colourful and profound tales of adventure. The men who influenced his formative years had no claim to fame in the conventional sense; what made them remarkable was the consuming desire they all shared to understand the deepest mysteries of life.

Working on Yourself Alone: Inner Dreambody Work
Arnold Mindell

Western psychotherapy and Eastern meditation are two contrasting ways of learning more about one's self. The first depends heavily on the powers of the therapist. *Process-oriented* meditation, however, can be used by the individual as a means of resolving conflicts and increasing awareness from within. Using meditation, dream work and yoga, this remarkable book offers techniques that you can develop on your own, allowing the growth of an individual method.

The Development of the Personality: Seminars in Psychological Astrology Volume I   Liz Greene and Howard Sasportas

Taking as a starting point their groundbreaking work on the cross-fertilization between astrology and psychology, Liz Greene and Howard Sasportas show how depth psychology works with the natal chart to illuminate the experiences and problems all of us encounter throughout the development of our individual identity, from childhood onwards.

Homage to the Sun: The Wisdom of the Magus of Strovolos
Kyriacos C. Markides

Homage to the Sun continues the adventure into the mysterious and extraordinary world of the spiritual teacher and healer Daskalos, the 'Magus of Strovolos'. The logical foundations of Daskalos' world of other dimensions are revealed to us – invisible masters, past-life memories and guardian angels, all explained by the Magus with great lucidity and scientific precision.

The Eagle's Gift   Carlos Castaneda

In the sixth book in his astounding journey into sorcery, Castaneda returns to Mexico. Entering once more a world of unknown terrors, hallucinatory visions and dazzling insights, he discovers that he is to replace the Yaqui Indian don Juan as leader of the apprentice sorcerers – and learns of the significance of the Eagle.

ARKANA – NEW-AGE BOOKS FOR MIND, BODY AND SPIRIT

A selection of titles

Being Intimate: A Guide to Successful Relationships
John Amodeo and Kris Wentworth

This invaluable guide aims to enrich one of the most important – yet often problematic – aspects of our lives: intimate relationships and friendships.

'A clear and practical guide to the realization and communication of authentic feelings, and thus an excellent pathway towards lasting intimacy and love' – George Leonard

Real Philosophy: An Anthology of the Universal Search for Meaning Jacob Needleman

It is only in addressing the huge, fundamental questions such as 'Who am I?' and 'Why death?' that humankind finds itself capable of withstanding the worst and abiding in the best. The selections in this book are a survey of that universal quest for understanding and are particularly relevant to the awakening taking place in the world today as old orders crumble. The authors call it Real Philosophy.

The Act of Creation Arthur Koestler

This second book in Koestler's classic trio of works on the human mind (which opened with *The Sleepwalkers* and concludes with *The Ghost in the Machine*) advances the theory that all creative activities – the conscious and unconscious processes underlying artistic originality, scientific discovery and comic inspiration – share a basic pattern, which Koestler expounds and explores with all his usual clarity and brilliance.

Whole in One: The Near-Death Experience and the Ethic of Interconnectedness David Lorimer

This prodigious study of the interconnectedness of creation draws on world-wide traditions of the after-life and detailed near-death experiences to posit an intrinsic moral order at work in the universe. 'This great book will take its permanent place in the literature of the spiritual renaissance in our time' – Sir George Trevelyan

ARKANA – NEW-AGE BOOKS FOR MIND, BODY AND SPIRIT

A selection of titles

A History of Magic Richard Cavendish

'Richard Cavendish can claim to have discovered the very spirit of magic' – *The Times Literary Supplement*. Magic has long enjoyed spiritual and cultural affiliations – Christ was regarded by many as a magician, and Mozart dabbled – as well as its share of darkness. Richard Cavendish traces this underground stream running through Western civilization.

One Arrow, One Life: Zen, Archery and Daily Life
Kenneth Kushner

When he first read Eugen Herrigel's classic *Zen in the Art of Archery* at college, Kenneth Kushner dismissed it as 'vague mysticism'; ten years later, he followed in Herrigel's footsteps along the 'Way of the Bow'. *One Arrow, One Life* provides a frank description of his training; while his struggles to overcome pain and develop spiritually, and the *koans* (or riddles) of his masters, illustrate vividly the central concepts of Zen.

City Shadows Arnold Mindell

'The shadow destroys cultures if it is not valued and its meaning not understood.' The city shadows are the repressed and unrealized aspects of us all, lived openly by the 'mentally ill'. In this compassionate book Arnold Mindell, founder of process-oriented psychology, presents the professionals of the crisis-ridden mental health industry with a new and exciting challenge.

In Search of the Miraculous: Fragments of an Unknown Teaching P. D. Ouspensky

Ouspensky's renowned, vivid and characteristically honest account of his work with Gurdjieff from 1915–18.

'Undoubtedly a *tour de force*. To put entirely new and very complex cosmology and psychology into fewer than 400 pages, and to do this with a simplicity and vividness that makes the book accessible to any educated reader, is in itself something of an achievement' – *The Times Literary Supplement*